DANCING WITH DINOSAURS

Dancing —*with*— Dinosaurs

Ministry in a Hostile and Hurting World

WILLIAM EASUM

Abingdon Press
Nashville

DANCING WITH DINOSAURS
MINISTRY IN A HOSTILE AND HURTING WORLD

Copyright © 1993 by Abingdon Press

Library of Congress Cataloging-in-Publication Data

ESAUM, WILLIAM M., 1939-
    Dancing with dinosaurs : ministry in a hostile and hurting world / William M. Easum.
        p.   cm.
    Includes bibliographical references.
    ISBN 0-687-31679-0 (pbk. : alk. paper)
    1. Pastoral theology. 2. Clergy—Office. 3. Protestant churches–United States. 4. United States—Church history—20th century.
    I. Title.
    BV4011.E328   1993
    253—dc20`   93-4029
                                                                CIP

99 00 01 02 03 04 05 06 07 08 — 20 19 18 17 16 15 14 13 12 11

MANUFACTURED IN THE UNITED STATES OF AMERICA

*To the many faithful Christians
who are wondering why ministries
that once discipled people
no longer work*

Contents

Preface:
Standing on the Threshold 9

CHAPTER 1:
Bursting Wineskins and Munching Sheep 11

CHAPTER 2:
Caught in a Crack of History 23

CHAPTER 3:
The Fringe People 37

CHAPTER 4:
Leading the Sheep Back to Pasture 45

CHAPTER 5:
The Demise of the Program-Based Church 57

CHAPTER 6:
A Reformation in Worship 81

CHAPTER 7:
What Ever Happened to the Sunday Church?   **97**

CHAPTER 8:
Three Essential Ingredients of Paradigm Communities   **107**

NOTES   **115**

Standing on the Threshold

*The unmotivated are notoriously
invulnerable to insight.*
EDWIN H. FRIEDMAN

One of my favorite musicals is *The Man of La Mancha.* Its two primary characters have captivated me throughout my ministry because they caricature the players in much of Protestantism's struggle for renewal: Don Quixote, dreamer of impossible dreams, the one who tilted at windmills, loved those unable to return his love, and dared to go where even the brave dared not go; and poor Sancho Panza, the eternal survivor, the faithful follower, who never dared to dream or initiate on behalf of something better.

Many Protestant leaders remind me of Sancho Panza. They are faithful. They are willing to struggle along, trying to manage what remains of their once great denomination, never willing to risk for the sake of the future, never dreaming of making a move toward the impossible dream.

But the spirit of Don Quixote lives on in many Protestant leaders. They dream of revitalized congregations and denominations even if it appears to be an impossible dream. They desire more than mere survival. They are passionate that their once great denomination must thrive again. They are willing to tilt at any windmill that blows them closer to the impossible dream.

I wonder who will win. I'm placing my money on the Don

Quixotes of this world. But then, I've chased a few impossible dreams before, and some of them have come true.

Put on your dreamer's cap and walk with me through a series of new paradigms that may open up new possibilities in the midst of old problems. Dare to dream as you read. Ask the Holy Spirit to be your guide on this journey. Above all, leave your religious hat at home and dare to ask God for new ways to achieve those eternal dreams.

Bill Easum
Port Aransas, Texas

CHAPTER 1

Bursting Wineskins and Munching Sheep

*O Lord, I pray, let the Lord go with us. Although this is a
stiff-necked people, pardon our iniquity and our sin.*

(EXOD. 34:9)

*He answered them, "And why do you break the
commandment of God for the sake of your tradition?"*

(MATT. 15:3)

Neither is new wine put into old wineskins.

(MATT. 9:17)

*Parables are often used when the raw truth is too strong to be
heard.*

There once was a woman who owned the finest winery in
all the land. Everything about the winery was superb. The fer-
tile land yielded some of the finest grapes to be found. The
large wooden vats that nurtured the crushed grapes until
maturity produced the world's most exquisite wine. For more
than two centuries people came from all over the world to
visit the winery and drink the famous wine.

One day the wine developed a bitter taste. No one could
explain why. Nothing had changed. The wine was still made
exactly as it had been made the last two centuries. Winery
visitors and customers began to decline. In desperation, the
woman hired consultants from all over the world to discover
the reason for the wine's sudden bitter taste. After days of
study, each expert arrived at the same diagnosis—the vats had
outlived their usefulness. They were old and sour with no way
of being cleaned and restored. The consultants concluded
that the woman's only option was to replace the old vats.

She was outraged. The beautiful vats had been in her family longer than she had. To the woman, family traditions were

11

more important than the decline of her winery. She made desperate attempts to improve her wine. She tried different fertilizers, changed the acidity of the ground, designed new labels on the bottles, and even hired a new overseer of the grapes. But she continued to put the wine into the old wooden vats. And the finest grapes in the world continued to produce bitter wine.

The number of the winery's visitors and customers continued to diminish until the day arrived when no one came to taste or buy the wine. The only remaining customers were the faithful members of the family for whom family traditions were more important than making satisfying wine.

The owner of the winery knew why the grapes were making bitter wine. She had all the knowledge she needed to restore her winery to its former glory. But she lacked the courage to use the knowledge at her disposal to make the changes necessary to produce satisfying wine like she had for years before. Family traditions ran too deep to replace the vats. In time the world famous vineyards fell into ruin, and only the family members continued to drink the bitter wine.

Jesus said, "Neither is new wine put into old wineskins; otherwise, the skins burst, and the wine is spilled, and the skins are destroyed; but new wine is put into fresh wineskins, and so both are preserved" (Matt. 9:17). The wineskin is the church. For two centuries North American congregations swiftly and efficiently spread the good news across this vast continent offering the grace of God to every part of North America. Today, many of these congregations are becoming irrelevant to a hurting unchurched world and are unable to offer new wine to the new generation.

This parable announces a warning to churches that look to the past and ignore the transitional signs all around them. God is calling us to find new ways to apply the good news to a new emerging world. Our churches often fail to quench the thirst of a spiritually dehydrated world. Churches with a slow pace of change are no longer adequate in a fast-changing world. Structures designed to coordinate ministry are unable to cause innovation. Ministries that worked in the industrial society no longer meet the spiritual needs of people in an informational society. In an age of computers, we cannot express truth in the language of a chariot age. The time has come for new wineskins.

Developing new wineskins requires that we learn a new language, understand new customs, and find new ways to make the timeless gospel relevant to our culture. And we must do so without diminishing the use of the word *Christian,* even in our pursuit of inclusiveness or ecumenism.

New Paradigms

This book offers new paradigms for ministry for an age that is indifferent and hostile toward Christianity.[1] A paradigm is a set of assumptions, beliefs, ideas, values, or expectations that form a filter through which we make meaning out of life, create structure and process, view information, and make value judgments. This filter contains the rules and regulations by which we see reality. A paradigm sets the boundaries in which we are willing to process information and tells us how to solve problems. Our paradigms are what allow us to accept or cause us to reject new ideas, or keep us from seeing information in a new way. Our paradigms must change if we are to understand what is happening today and help shape the future.

Twelve assumptions will form a filter for the ideas in this book. By sharing them, I in no way convey that these assumptions are the only way to filter reality. As we will see later, however, these assumptions form the filter through which many of today's most effective pastors sift reality.

1. North America is the new mission field.
2. Society will become increasingly hostile toward Christianity in the twenty-first century.

13

3. The distinction between clergy and laity will disappear in the twenty-first century.

4. If churches only improve what they have been doing, they will die.

5. The best way to fail today is to improve yesterday's successes.

6. Bureaucracies and traditional practices are the major causes of the decline of most denominations in North America.

7. Traditional churches that thrive in the twenty-first century will initiate radical changes before the year 2001.

8. God exists and creates everything.

9. Jesus Christ is the center of all human life.

10. The Bible is our primary source of faith and practice.

11. The purpose of the Body of Christ is to bring the world to faith in Jesus Christ.

12. A way will be found to avoid world ecological and economic disaster.

If these twelve assumptions composed the filter through which you approached ministry, what changes would you consider making in the style or tasks of your ministry? For the moment, set aside traditional practices and the personal assumptions on which you have done ministry, and take a fresh, objective look at new paradigms for ministry. *I am not proposing that the substance of the gospel be changed. I am proposing that we need to radically change the way we package and proclaim the substance of the gospel.* Making a few adjustments here and there will not help. If we simply do better what we are presently doing in our old wine vats, we will continue to be irrelevant and, in time, extinct.

Dancing with Dinosaurs

Congregations whose membership has plateaued or is declining have much in common with dinosaurs. Both have great heritages. Both require enormous amounts of food.

Both influenced their world tremendously. And both became endangered species. Will many of our congregations, like the dinosaurs, become extinct?

No one knows scientifically why dinosaurs became extinct, so this analogy might be helpful. Notice the dinosaur in the picture. Perhaps the vegetation previously grew much higher than depicted in the picture. Over time the plant growth was stunted by the dinosaur's tremendous appetite.

Still, food was plentiful if the dinosaur merely bent down to reach the vegetation. But perhaps the dinosaur's neck was too stiff to bend down to the vegetation, or the dinosaur was too nearsighted to see the vegetation. Perhaps dinosaurs became extinct because of their unwillingness or inability to see what was happening all around them.

Many congregations today have the same problem. Like the dinosaur, they have a voracious appetite. Much of their time, energy, and money is spent foraging for food, so that little time is left to feed the unchurched. And faced with a radically changing world, many are unwilling to feed where they have never fed before. Either their pride or their nearsightedness keeps them from changing the ways they minister to people. And they are running out of food. White upper-middle-income Anglican Protestants are declining; the world is becoming culturally and racially diverse and unchurched.

All around are unchurched, hurting people. America has a far greater population today than when Protestantism was at its peak in 1964. Food is everywhere. But many refuse to change their methods and structures to minister to people where they are in ways they can understand. Like the dinosaur, their necks are too stiff or their eyes too nearsighted.

Clearly, God doesn't care if these congregations survive; but God passionately cares if they meet the spiritual needs of those God sends their way. Congregations must deal with their stiff necks or their nearsightedness, or go the way of the dinosaur.

Figure 1

THE VISION

NEW LIFE COMES TO US

ON ITS WAY

TO SOMEONE ELSE

Figure 2

This book proposes that clergy and laity can retool traditional, dying churches so that they can dance with dinosaurs. This dance will not be easy, but we must find new ways to pass on the old message. We must learn how to minister in a radically new world if we plan to rescue the church from its approaching demise.

New life comes to us on its way to someone else: If we pass it on to others, we blossom and grow; if we keep it to ourselves, we wither and die. This is the message of the gospel in a nutshell. We must teach the dinosaurs of our churches how to dance to its tune.[2]

Culturally relevant and Christ-focused congregations are designed and structured to introduce people to Christ in a language that they can understand and respond to with integrity. These congregations use the tools and vehicles offered by culture to pass on the new life in Christ. Most congregations will have to discontinue or do differently much of what they are doing today to accomplish such a mission. It is for this reason that most of the effective congregations of the future have not yet been started.

Why, then, do some churches allow this new life to stop with them? Why are so many churches focused more on themselves than on Christ and the world? How can some people be content going to meetings and taking care of facilities? How did we drift so far from our original mandate from our Lord to "go therefore and make disciples of all nations . . ." (Matt. 28:19).

The Munching Sheep Theory

My first pastorate was in sheep country, so I learned a lot about sheep. They have a habit of getting so involved in feeding themselves that they munch along for hours without looking up to see where they are going. All is well, as long as the sheep munch in their own pasture. But if a gate is left open, sheep are known to munch their way through the gate onto the adjacent highway, and many are run over by passing motorists without ever knowing what hit them, or why.

Many of us have slowly munched our way so far from our roots that we do not realize how far removed we are from who we once were. Our present decline is not the result of poor intentions or intentional decisions to be unfaithful. Our intentions are good and we desire to be faithful. We have merely convinced ourselves that who we are today is who we have always been.

Our task is to discern between present traditional practices and our Christian roots. We must rediscover and reclaim our spiritual heritage. The emerging new world of the twenty-first century may be new to us, but it is not new to our spiritual ancestors. They developed Christian community in the midst of a very similar culture. If by God's grace, they could do it, so can we.

Excuses

Christians are commissioned to witness to the life, death, and resurrection of Jesus Christ. The church of Jesus Christ is "called out of the world" in order to be equipped to go back into the world for the purpose of sharing new life. Every mandate left by our Lord focused on this mission. No congregation is exempt. Nurturing members of the church for the sake of those members alone is not the mission of the church. It does not matter how small or large the congregation is; the mission is still the same. The purpose of the church is to win the world to faith in God through Jesus Christ. The purpose of the pastor is to equip people to build up the Body of Christ. The purpose of laity is to pass on to others the new life God has given them. The goal is never simply to "run the church," no matter what size the church may be.

Typical negative responses to this bias are varied: "I pastor a church that simply cannot grow because of its location"; "I believe that a small church is better than a large church";

"God did not call me to be an evangelist; counseling is my emphasis"; "I believe that quality is more important than quantity"; "I serve a very old, small congregation. All I can do is to love them"; "I am not willing to prostitute the gospel for the sake of numbers."

Each response is an excuse to avoid responding to the primary call of God to the church of Jesus Christ—to disciple the world.

The congregation that cannot grow because of its location can (1) move to a new location; (2) join with one or two other churches in selling all the property and begin a new congregation with a new name; (3) stay where it is and help start a new congregation in an area close enough that it can help others.

The congregation that wishes to remain small can (1) send members out to start a new congregation in areas of population growth and attract new converts to replace those sent out to start the new congregation; (2) provide the money and expertise to help start new congregations without sending any new members because they are in a rapidly decreasing population.

Very old, small congregations can (1) reach out to the nursing homes; (2) do work at home for other congregations in the area that are growing; (3) send money to help start new congregations.

The pastor whose primary skill is that of counseling may use counseling as a way to help people grow in their ability to reach out to others.[3]

The person who is concerned about quality versus quantity needs to read the Acts of the Apostles. The Bible never pits the two measures against each other.

And those who are not willing to prostitute the gospel for the sake of growth need to read this book very carefully, because nothing could be farther from my mind when I conclude that if the Body of Christ were truly the Body of Christ, it would grow. Nowhere do I read that integrity has to be sacrificed in order for Christianity to grow.

Size is not the issue. We need both strong small and strong large congregations that exist for others. No matter who we are or what size congregation we are a part of, our role is to be a culturally relevant, Christ-focused people. We never get too old or too small to carry out the mission of telling others the good news that Jesus Christ has come to bring us abundant life. It is up to the leadership to find ways to pass on the new life no matter what the circumstances.

How to Get the Most Out of This Book

First, the words *church, congregation, community* or *communities,* and *tradition* are used in specific ways. *Church* is used to denote the normal, decaying, "out of touch" church. It is never used in a flattering or positive way. *Congregation* is a neutral term that denotes neither positive or negative thoughts. *Community* (or *communities*) is always a positive reference about healthy, growing congregations, present or future. *Tradition* is always used negatively. It is not to be confused with *heritage. Heritage* can be compared to the Ten Commandments and *tradition* includes the vast lists of legal rules, regulations, and interpretations that were added later.

Next, you need to know that the endnotes contain a wealth of information about resources that can be used in a local congregation. This information is placed in the endnotes to avoid breaking the flow of thought. If you resonate with a particular section of the book, then turn to the endnotes for more information.

Finally, if something in this book offends you, before you get mad or decide to stop reading, ask yourself this question: Am I offended because what I've read attacks my basic theological and biblical underpinnings, or am I offended because what I have read challenges one of my personal assumptions, sacred cows, or traditions? Knowing the difference may prove difficult, but making such a distinction is a major agenda of our era.

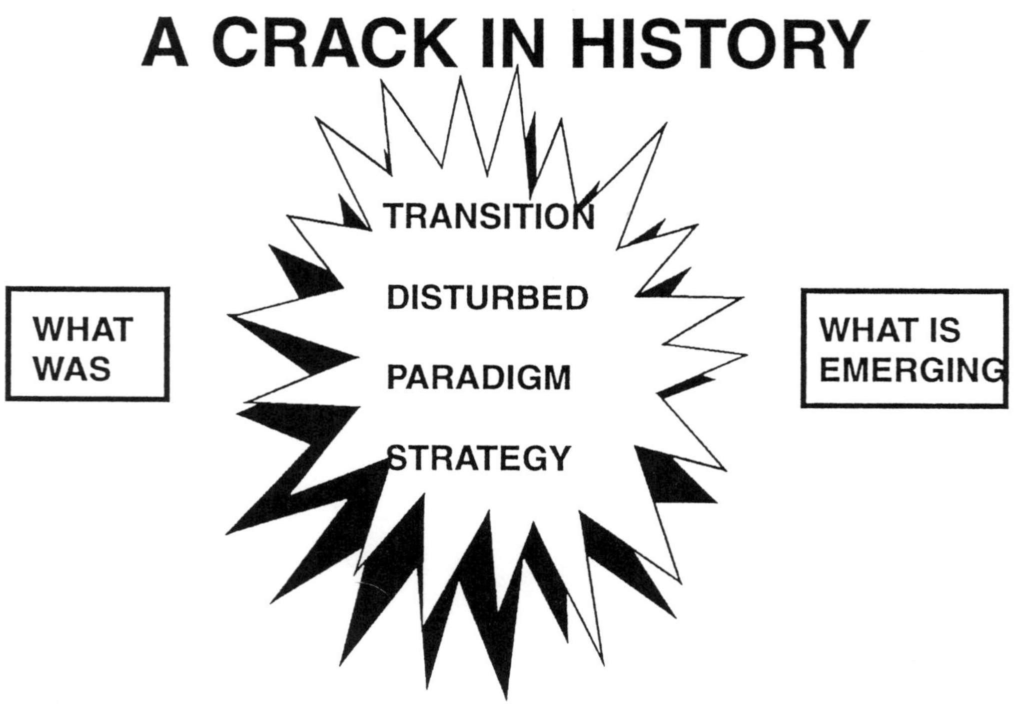

A CRACK IN HISTORY

WHAT
WAS

TRANSITION
DISTURBED
PARADIGM
STRATEGY

WHAT IS
EMERGING

Figure 3

CHAPTER 2

Caught in a Crack
of History

You have to see the future to deal with the present.
                                        FAITH POPCORN

*The planet is falling percipiently apart and coming
together again at the very same moment.*
                                        BENJAMIN R. BARBER[1]

*North America is caught in the crack between what was and what
is emerging.* This crack began opening in 1960 and will close
sometime around the year 2014. Trusted values held for centuries are falling into this crack, never to be seen again. Ideas
and methodologies that once worked no longer achieve the
desired results. This crack in our history is so enormous that
it is causing a metamorphosis in every area of life. The 1990s
are often called "the hinge of history" or the "transforming
boundary between one age and another, between a scheme
of things that has disintegrated and another that is taking
shape."[2] But I call the 1990s "a crack of history."

Sixteen paradigm shifts are occurring as we move through
this crack. These shifts are not fads that will soon pass. They
have worldwide social, economic, and political significance.
These shifts are interrelated and have a profound effect on
one another.[3] Collectively, these shifts are recreating our perception of reality. Today, the fastest way to fail is to improve
upon yesterday's successes.[4]

These paradigm shifts are now the focus of conversation for
leaders who wish to reach this new emerging world with new
life in Christ. These conversations are challenging the basic
values that once gave meaning and substance to our lives. They

are the springboards for developing new ministries and missions that pass on the timeless gospel. These paradigm shifts allow us the opportunity to look into the crack, to see old familiar things in new ways, and to devise new ways to accomplish our divine mandate to make disciples of all nations.

Figure 4 charts these shifts. These shifts do not forecast the future. Instead, they are assumptions that form the paradigm out of which we take action, knowing that our actions can shape the future. How religious communities respond to these shifts will determine their future and the level of humanity in the new emerging world.

Figure 4

What Was	The Crack in History	The Shift	The Emerging World
Ecclesiastical	Nonecclesiastical	Laity/Priesthood	?
Churched	Unchurched	Hostility	?
Discovery	Discernment	Truth	?
Modern	Postmodern	Technology	?
Corporate	Individual	Broken	?
Institutional	Noninstitutional	Relational	?
Bureaucratic	Entrepreneurial	Risk Taking	?
Middle Class	High & Low	Redirected	?
National	Pacific Rim	Global	?
Neighborhood	Regional	Large	?
Print	Sight & Sound	Visual	?
Centralized	Decentralized	Structure	?
Industrial	Informational	Process	?
White	Ethnic	Diverse	?
Male	Female	Inclusive	?
Obligation	Compassion	Meaning	?

As you read through these shifts, ask yourself, What are the implications for my ministry?

Shift One

During this crack in history, North America is moving from a society dominated by clerics to a society where the laity dominate the church. Three events are precipitating this change. First, the rediscovery of the Bible discloses the fallacy of the role presently played by the clergy. Second, over the next ten to fifteen years large numbers of the present clergy will retire or die and replacements will not fill the void. Third, discretionary income among the middle class continues to dwindle, making it increasingly difficult to staff congregations adequately.

In the emerging world the marginalization of the laity will end, and the role of ordained clergy will disappear. The priesthood of the believer will emerge as the dominant force in congregations. Clergy will equip laity to live out their roles as priests.

Shift Two

During the crack in history, North America is moving from a churched to an unchurched society. North America is becoming the new mission field. Presently, this new mission field is ignoring Christianity because it is not perceived as a threat to commerce. But the new emerging world will become increasingly anti-Christian and will try to rid itself of Christianity.[5] Christian bashing is one of the few remaining discriminations acceptable in the twenty-first century.[6] On numerous occasions, Lyle Schaller, one of the most prominent congregational consultants, has raised numerous concerns about the long-term effects of government intervention into the life of the church. He suggests that some denominations need to fund a good test case in the courts regarding the first and fourth amendments.[7]

The media will increasingly launch attacks against Christian values.[8] Local residents will ask churches to leave their neighborhoods, and government agencies will attempt to tax the church. Television sitcoms will continue to bash Christian values. As Christianity and culture continue to separate and finally divorce in the emerging world, disdain for Christians will continue to escalate.

The further we journey into the new emerging world the more society will struggle to define what it means by the words *religious* and *spiritual*. In the crack of history, the Judeo-Christian worldview will be severely tested by government attempts to define what is religious for the purpose of taxing. The Judeo-Christian worldview will also face the growing challenge of the New Age, naturalistic humanism, naturalism, scientism, mysticism, and technologism.[9] The new mission field will find the Christian God just one god among many. Few of these gods will appear as tempting and promising as the god of technology. A prime example began in 1988, when a two-hundred-million-dollar-a-year project called the Human Genome Initiative was launched to develop a recipe for making a human being.[10]

Shift Three

The age of discovery is over; the age of discernment is beginning. While the crack remains open, society will experience a shift from innovation to application. The last three decades have produced so many discoveries that we may spend the next fifty years sorting through the facts and figuring out the combinations made possible by these discoveries. Applying the newly discovered technologies will bring about new life-styles, new ways of transmitting and assimilating knowledge, and new ways of performing tasks at home and the workplace.[11] Fundamental changes are taking place in concepts once thought to be sacred. In the crack, time issues are no longer one dimensional, and decision making processes are becoming more complex. In the emerging world, whoever controls information controls power.

Shift Four

Few people will believe in any form of ultimate truth in the emerging world because the definition of truth is changing. Prior to this crack in history, truth was defined by religion and faith. If the Bible seemed to conflict with the way we perceived reality, our perception was in error. In the crack, truth is determined by science, but the emerging world will not define truth by science.[12] Instead, the shift toward pragmatism, begun by William James in the early part of this century and supported by John Dewey, has come to fruition. Truth will be defined by whatever works. Technology will be the new god that defines truth.

The primary task of technology will be the preservation of the totality of the planet for economic reasons (econ-ecofaith as opposed to biocentric or ecofaith) and North America's way of life (bioethics).[13] The holistic health of the person and the planet will become the primary challenge of society. Medical ethics will find its greatest challenge when technology discovers how to transplant the brain. The supremacy of the sovereign God will be balanced against the capability of human technology to do good or evil. Major studies are already underway to discover the pathways to understanding how the brain functions.

Shift Five

Moral standards are like chameleons in the crack—constantly in the state of change. Sin continues to be outdated.[14] Children's values vary depending on the values of their daycare workers and are challenged by the cynical world of *MTV*. Concern for the common good is disappearing. In the crack the individual is the king or the queen.[15] People are preoccupied with themselves. Whatever is done behind closed doors is considered acceptable conduct. Privacy is the ultimate prize.[16] In the new emerging society right or wrong will not

27

exist. Whatever benefits the individual will form the basis for ethics. Such shifts are natural in a world where truth is defined by technology.

The family will be the place where ethics change the most. Presently, the United States Census Bureau defines family as a group of two or more persons related by birth, marriage, or adoption residing together. In the emerging world, the family will be defined as any group of two or more people who intentionally live together for the purpose of loving and caring for each other regardless of gender or time commitment. It will not be considered normal to live a lifetime with one spouse. People will marry solely for what they personally can gain from it.[17] "Serial monogamy" will become the norm.

Without any constant center to hold on to, most people will be broken, stressed out, and disjointed. Studies already show that people who live together before marriage are more likely to get a divorce.[18] Eight out of ten people already experience some form of abuse. Self-help books fill the bookstores. Addiction to one drug or another describes the life-style of over half of the population.[19] In the emerging world, virtual reality, which allows users to see and experience places and events as though they were actually present, will become the new power drug of the rich,[20] and AIDS will threaten the fabric of society especially among minorities and adolescents and will change our patterns of behavior for decades.

Shift Six

Belonging is more important than joining while in the crack of history. Instead of trusting institutions people are bonding with groups of people who provide the kind of relationships that meet their individual needs. The emerging world will bring about the decline of all institutions even if they are well endowed.

Safety and a sense of security will become more important than risk taking.[21] The majority of people will tend to withdraw physically and psychologically. People will continue to move to the suburbs. Small, secure groups will become the primary form of socializing. People will trust individuals more than systems of thought or institutions.

Shift Seven

More knowledge, appropriated faster than ever before, will make for more unpredictability in the crack. Speed will rival quality. Fluctuations in everything are becoming greater than ever before. Red tape is being reduced to a minimum. Organizations are streamlining everything for faster response to the customer. Therefore, bureaucracies, secular and religious, will have a hard time in the intermediate future; but entrepreneurs will do well. In the emerging society, leaders will be those willing to risk leaving the safety of the "good-ole-boy" system. Those who remain tied to a bureaucracy will be lost. Institutions that cling to their bureaucracies will vanish.

Amoeba-like organizations will fill the twenty-first century landscape. These organizations will be adaptive and flexible, able to change overnight. The organizations will be geared toward learning as much as producing. Those who learn the most will produce the most in the emerging world.

Shift Eight

The illusion of wealth is disappearing during the crack. The average family's income is steadily declining, the ranks of the poor steadily increasing, and the middle class continues to shrink in size.[22] Businesses that focus on the middle class are experiencing shrinking profits. Those that focus their attention on either the high or the low end of the marketplace will be the performers of the emerging world.

As it disappears, the middle class will become more and more hostile toward anyone and anything threatening their neighborhoods or their way of life with pollution or overdevelopment. Organizations that cause traffic congestion or noise pollution will be asked to leave middle class communities. Already the Clean Up generation (baby busters) resent the life-style of the baby boomer.[23]

Shift Nine

The end of the cold war, the rise of the Pacific Rim, and the continual movement toward a European currency is redefining the traditional role played by nations and superpowers in the crack of history. A global economy is redefining nationalism.[24] In the emerging world, each nation will be given a role to play in the world economy. America will become the guardian of peace, selling its military might to protect the rest of the world. Global National Products will replace Gross National Products. A global stock market will network and in time merge with national stock markets. A global life-style will emerge that involves food, travel, films, fashion, language, and human rights.[25] The interconnectedness of the economy will almost eliminate wars, and a world government will be established.

Shift Ten

In the crack of history, North America's fascination with the automobile and travel has diminished the emphasis on neighborhoods and will lead to the development of a regional mentality. Today, very few North Americans eat, play, or socialize in the neighborhood where they live. In the emerging new world, many people will eat, play, socialize, and work in the same locale. "Edge cities" are already developing for those who can afford to live in them.[26] The role of the city will continue to decline. In time, cities will be dismantled altogether.

Shift Eleven

Sights and sounds dominate the crack of history. The arts, typically enjoyed by the more affluent and educated, and entertainment, normally enjoyed by the masses, will become merged. Interactive television will become the way we perceive, assimilate, and interpret news and reality. The use of print continues to disappear and change. The majority of print that does survive will be electronic. Children will read books on computers and creatively change the story as they read. In the new emerging world the media will finally become the message. If something cannot be seen and experienced, it will not be heard or accepted.[27]

Shift Twelve

Decentralization is required in the crack of history. A return to grass roots participation will cause the restructuring of every aspect of organizational life. Corporations will give employees more authority. Team work, diversity, and an emphasis on creativity will become the primary method of profitability.[28] Giant monoliths will be replaced with webs of smaller enterprises that are encapsuled inside large businesses for accounting purposes.[29] Corporate executives will have to be comfortable in a vast array of different corporate structures that span the globe, and they will have to be bilingual. In the emerging new society, villages, edge cities, provinces, counties, regions, and states will again gain more power than the federal government. And this miniaturization will actually speed up the drive for a world economy.[30]

Shift Thirteen

In the crack of history, the transmission and reception of knowledge and information are experiencing a series of quantum leaps.[31] Computers are totally changing the way we

31

treat knowledge. Presently, a productive person knows how to get, use, develop, and share knowledge. In the emerging world, knowing how to process knowledge, rather than collecting, storing and retrieving knowledge, will be the primary skill.[32] People will have less need of memory or writing skills. Knowledge will be processed purely from a global perspective. Sequential, linear, rational, deductive thinking will continue to disappear. Many affluent people will begin to rely too much on artificial intelligence and many people on the economic fringes will think less.[33]

Home schooling and private schools will continue to grow in the emerging world until they comprise the majority of the thinking population. In time, public schools will be replaced by the private sector, funded by the government and businesses. Many of these will be religious schools.[34]

Shift Fourteen

By the year 2001, one in four people in America will be nonwhite, making the emerging society the most diverse ever.[35] Today, the new culturally disadvantaged are those white young people raised in the suburbs who are able to converse in only one language. The emerging world will be no longer dominated by white, Anglo-Saxon Protestants. White-skinned North Americans will experience the same kind of negative treatment they gave to those of different colored skin. Interracial marriages will produce many of North American babies born in the emerging world.

Shift Fifteen

The male-dominated world is disappearing in the crack of history. In the emerging society, the "glass ceiling" that has kept women out of top-level jobs will disappear. According to John Naisbett, women have already established themselves in the industries of the future.[36] Inclusiveness will replace sexism in the job market; male roles will be redefined and lessened in importance. A new set of women's values will dominate all areas of life.[37] Day care, maternity/paternity leave, and full- and part-time jobs both at home and away will become common employee benefits.

Shift Sixteen

In the crack of history, characteristics such as obligation and duty are being replaced with compassion and empathy. The Protestant work ethic is being replaced with an emphasis on fulfillment and personal meaning. Life-styles and work standards are becoming more relaxed. The crack presents people with so many choices that even though they work fewer hours than ever before, they do not have time to do everything they want to do.

The emerging world will experience a clash between a need for quality products and a passion for a more relaxed life-style. Individuals who choose to work hard rather than enjoy a more relaxed life-style will do well. Those who choose to play will not do well.

A Window of Opportunity

Together, these sixteen paradigm shifts form the context for ministry today and open windows of opportunity to future ministries.[38] New forms of ministry, woven out of the fabric of each of these major shifts, will provide ministry in the emerging world. The key to understanding their meaning for Christian congregations is in seeing them not as individual shifts that stand alone, but in realizing that they form a set of assumptions that are producing a new paradigm for the emerging world. The churches that unlock, retool themselves, and act upon the implications running back and forth between these shifts will develop new ministries and structures that bring about a new and more effective alignment of the physical and spiritual resources of humanity. They will grow in spirit and numbers and will be prepared for ministry in the twenty-first century.

Congregations that resist or ignore these paradigm shifts will continue to die. Pastors who do not retool will work harder and harder and become less and less effective. Pastors, laity, and denominational leaders need to act now.

The actions needed today require wisdom and courage. What may seem impossible today will be the norm tomorrow. The information we have to work with changes so fast that it is impossible to guarantee which ministry will be successful. Leaders need to trust their instincts. And that proves fatal when our personal assumptions remain unchanged. Where, then, can we turn for help to form a new paradigm?

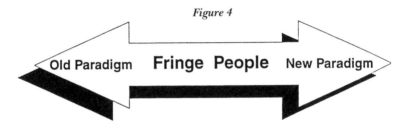

Figure 4

The Future Is on the Fringe

The shape of the future is always on the fringe of normality during times of paradigm shifts. The changes are so immense and so encompassing that no one really knows where they are taking our planet in the twenty-first century. Only one thing is certain—nothing is normal. Who, then, do we turn to when looking for clues about ministry in the twenty-first century? We certainly cannot turn to those who insist on clinging to the status quo. We turn to the people on the fringe of normalcy.

Fringe people, who develop nontraditional ministries, are

often looked upon as mavericks. But they point the way to the future. It is necessary to look at their work at the edges of the crack to determine where the shifts are taking society and what the new paradigms will look like. They are the prophets of tomorrow, and we must listen to what they are saying even if they make us uncomfortable. Many of these fringe people are documented in this chapter.

William McKinney explains:

> The old denominations have no hope of reaching out to the new populations of America—to people of color, to those drawn to the TV preachers, to those who struggle to make ends meet—if they remain bound to the notion that it is either possible or desirable to restore our churches to their earlier position of dominance. It is only when we accept the fact that our own new off-centeredness that we will have a chance to partnership with peoples whose current experience is also not of the center but of the margins.[39]

CHAPTER 3

The Fringe People

Adversity is often the window of opportunity for change. Few people or organizations want to change when there is prosperity and peace. Major changes are often precipitated by necessity.

LEIF ANDERSON

I think there is a world market for about five computers.

THOMAS J. WATSON
CHAIRMAN IBM, 1943

In every period of major transition, two kinds of leadership surface: those consumed by the threats of transition, and those open to the opportunities that always accompany transition. (See figure 3.)

Consider the reaction of religious leaders on the day of Pentecost. A new age was proclaimed, but the Pharisees and the devout Jews of every nation saw the day of Pentecost as a threat and dismissed the phenomenon as nothing more than a drunken orgy. As spiritual freedom spread, their resistance grew (Acts 2:5-12).

Many Christian leaders today are so consumed by the threats presented by the crack in history that they are paralyzed to see the opportunities taking shape in this crack in history. Some insist on clinging to the ways of the past; others yearn to recreate the past; most refuse to admit that the world they grew up in no longer exists.

However, many congregations have their share of people who are ready and able to give leadership in the crack in history. These are the fringe people, who are willing to concentrate on the opportunities rather than the threats. They have a holy discontent with the way things are. Fringe people know that if people are allowed to get too comfortable with the present, they learn to live in the past.

Fringe people make three assumptions. First assumption: *Everything that our churches and denominations are doing no longer*

37

works. They erase all of their preconceived ideas about the nature and mission of Christian congregations. They ask: What are the things congregations do today that no longer make sense? Why do we insist on doing them? What are the implications of not doing them? Is it possible to redirect them toward relevant, redemptive ministries?

Second assumption: *Things that most people think are impossible are possible.* They ask: What can we make possible today in our ministry to make our congregations more vital and relevant tomorrow?

Third assumption: *We live in a non-Christian society.* They are not afraid to use the phrase *non-Christian.* They know that the context in which congregations do ministry today is often Christian versus non-Christian. Based on these three assumptions, fringe people do the following:

Fringe people are servant leaders instead of professionals. An article appeared in the May 4, 1992, edition of *Fortune Magazine* entitled "The Leader As Servant."[1] Several of the idols of the 1980s such as Donald Trump and Lee Iacocca have fallen from grace. The leadership of the 1990s will be less grandiose. In fact, Robert Greenleaf's work of twenty years ago *Servant Leadership* will be freshly appreciated. The servant leader takes people and their work seriously, listens and takes the lead from the grass roots, heals when he or she can, is self-effacing, and sees himself or herself as a steward.

Fringe people gather, analyze, and understand the available information. The technological advancements of the 1960s have resulted in an unprecedented ability to gather, store, and retrieve information. Knowing how to use this information is determining the success of every organization in North America.

We know many things about our congregations. We know that (1) memberships are declining; (2) Sunday schools are declining; (3) mission programs are dwindling; (4) total memberships are growing older each year; (5) over the next twenty-five years the vast majority of our present membership will no longer be able to attend worship because of their age; (6) young adults are returning to organized religion in record numbers but few are found in our churches; (7) the majority of the present pastors are scheduled to retire in the next fifteen years; (8) time is now as much a god among young adults as was money for the previous generation; (9) healthy, neighborhood churches are a rarity; (10) sixty-six percent of women with children work outside the home; (11) church nurseries are in shambles; (12) tenure is rendering our seminaries irrelevant; (13) most of our members do not know nor understand the Bible much less have the skill to apply its principles to their decision making in the church; (14) the automobile has changed the way people come to church; (15) fewer teenagers are found in our services; (16) the number of children in Sunday school continues to fall.

Fringe people collect most of their data from outside their organizations rather than from within. They do not allow existing conditions such as their capabilities, location, strengths, weaknesses, and executive whims to determine the nature of their ministries. Instead they look outside the congregation or denomination to discover what ministries they need to develop.

One negative example of not looking outward for clues for developing new ministries happened while conducting a consultation with a local congregation surrounded by a huge single population. I said to them, "You really need to start a singles ministry." To which they responded, "Why? We don't have any singles in our church."

Fringe people look outside for clues to the future. They avoid the following four deadly sins of inside-out thinking: (1) complacency—"if it ain't broke don't fix it"; (2) blindness to the paradigm shifts occurring all around them; (3) megalomania—a one-person show that relies on intuition; (4) pride—going for the short-term quick fix while ignoring the long term.[2]

Fringe people have the courage to act on the available information, even if it means destroying traditional practices. Knowing the facts is not enough; leaders must be willing to act on the facts. Such action requires moral character and a willingness to make strategic decisions that will kill many of their own sacred cows. These leaders allow mission to win out over tradition.[3]

Fringe people master and teach the elements of excellence, innovation, and anticipation. Excellence is essential for any congregation to be competitive in an age when many forces pull people away from organized religion. Innovation is necessary if congregations are going to provide the new ministries for the new emerging world. Anticipation is required for congregations to be prepared to meet the fast changing needs of people in the crack in history.[4]

Fringe people know that one of the most important challenges in the crack in history is to free congregations from the chains of tradition.[5] Tradition assumes that the experiences of one generation are the norm for each succeeding generation. But traditions that brought new life to one generation may not do so for succeeding generations. For some, traditions become meaningless from one generation to another. For others, traditions begin to take the place of faith itself.

Jesus challenged the traditions of his day when he plucked grain on the Sabbath in full view of the Pharisees, knowing it was against the Jewish law. He knew that he was living in a time when everything was coming to an end and a new world was emerging. Many traditions had to be discarded if new life was to be passed on to others. Jesus sets the pattern fringe people seek to follow.

Fringe people are willing to practice triage. In the midst of war, nurses and doctors are forced to separate the wounded who have no hope of living from those who have a chance to live; they spend their time helping the latter. Those performing triage make mistakes in their evaluations sometimes, but if they refuse to do triage at all, fewer people will survive the war.[6]

Triage is necessary if we are to produce congregations that can pass on new life in Christ. We simply do not have the resources, time, or people to patronize congregations that focus their ministries on themselves. Some ministries within a congregation have a chance at reaching people whereas other efforts do not. Knowing the difference is the main task of congregational leaders. Some congregations have a chance at reaching people for Jesus Christ; some do not. Knowing the difference is a key task of denominational leaders.

The vital signs are simple during triage. Is the congregation willing to focus ministry primarily on passing on the new life in Christ, or is the church focused primarily on its own survival? Fringe people support those ministries and congregations willing to focus outward and allow those who insist on focusing inward to die with dignity. It is that simple for fringe people who are performing spiritual triage.

Triage will result in two categories of healthy Christ-focused communities in the twenty-first century. Some will be strong small communities focused outward; others will be strong large communities focused outward. A vast wasteland will exist in between. The inward-focused small and large church will disappear.

In the new emerging world, the strong small communities will consist of one service of worship with less than two hundred people. They will develop "niche" ministries for people mostly over fifty years of age with no children living at home. These two hundred people are warm and outgoing, and they love Christ more than the buildings or money in the bank. Retirement is not used as an excuse to quit sharing new life with others. Many wonderful spiritual, physical, and emotional needs are filled by the loving ministries of these people. Control and power are not part of their vocabulary. They have discovered the secret of life—*those who give away life are those who live.*

The strong large communities of the new emerging world

consist of multiple services, spread out during the week, totaling more than six hundred in worship.[7] The majority are found in metropolitan areas.[8] The people are young and old, rich and poor, with and without children, married and single, and of all ethnic backgrounds. The participants live out the gospel in the workplace. These communities are "teaching stations" where young pastors learn the skills needed to pastor in a strong large community. Other congregations come to them for guidance and support. Their ministries occur both on the property and in the workplace. They may worship at more than one site. They provide ministries seven days a week every month of the year. They are known by their distinctive logo and ministries, not by their denominational affiliation. They emphasize the new life that comes through faith in Jesus Christ rather than membership in the church. They encourage the use of their facilities instead of keeping them spotless. They have a Christian school from the cradle through elementary or high school that is a ministry for the purpose of bringing new life to the children and their parents. Those who worship regularly attend from all over the area. The services are indigenous to the style of music and custom of the area. Preaching is focused on how to live a Christian life seven days a week in a hostile world.

The congregations that have the best chance to become strong large Christ-focused communities in the twenty-first century are those that presently have a critical mass at worship of four hundred fifty.[9] They are large enough now to provide ministries to children, youth, and both single and married adults. These congregations have adequate land to accomplish many forms of weekday ministries, or the capacity to lease or purchase additional land, or the will to move.

Fringe people use two primary tools in developing congregations in the crack in history. One tool is an understanding of history and how it relates to understanding the future. The other tool is a willingness to use culture as a conduit or vehicle for conveying the historic message of the good news.

Our task now is to examine the historic roots of the Christian faith and the ministries of the effective fringe people of our time. As we do so, ask yourself, Is this a picture of the congregation where I serve Christ?

CHAPTER 4

Leading the Sheep
Back to Pasture

....

Never let go of what you've got until you've got hold of something else.
LANCE MORROW

We are the first generation of immigrant North Americans to live in a society that no longer appreciates the presence of Christianity.

A close comparison can be drawn between the challenge facing congregations today and the situation in which the Disciples found themselves after Jesus died. The early church shared the gospel in a religious, but hostile world. They faced an entirely new world. Caught in the crack between the ending of an age of law and the beginning of an age of the spirit, they were confused, disturbed, angry, sad, and alone.

The 1990s are bringing Christianity full circle. We have lived most of our lives in a friendly environment where Judeo-Christian values were either the accepted standards for living or at least respected as a way of life, but no longer. Today we live in a hostile mission field similar to the first century.

This change in the relationship between the church and culture is chronicled in many secular commentaries on our times. One of the words Alvin Toffler uses to describe the "edge of the 21st Century" is *violence*.[1] The *Wall Street Journal* had a lengthy article on the changing role of neighborhoods toward local churches. The headline sums up the article: "Here is the church; as for the people, they're pick-

45

eting it. Towns view new churches as bell-ringing eyesores; And all those weddings." [2]

Twisting and turning in the crack between the age that was and the age that is emerging, Christians need to rediscover the distinctive element of the first-century communities.

To develop culturally relevant, Christ-focused congregations, we must reexamine the life and ministry of the early church through eyes uncontaminated by an institutional or denominational mindset. Therefore, this study is limited to the first-century communities before institutional Christianity developed.[3]

We start with the Acts of the Apostles. We assume that the author included the salient events in the life of the first-century communities. Our goal is to discover themes in the early church before the institutional traditions of the so-called apostolic fathers began to dominate the religious scene.[4]

The Early Christian Communities

The Acts of the Apostles reveals four essential concerns around which the rest of the New Testament communities revolved. First, the early Christians came together to celebrate God through prayer, support, and teaching about the Way,[5] fasted, held everything in common, set leaders aside for certain ministries by laying hands on them, and counted and celebrated the addition of new people into the church.

Second, the early Christians went out to the Temple and into the streets to be witnesses to the life, death, and resurrection of Jesus Christ. Their message included entrance into the kingdom of God instead of a church, repentance from sin, and the personal experience of salvation. The power that sent them out to preach and teach was the Holy Spirit. Everywhere they went miracles occurred, and the people looked on in wonder. They existed to reach out and share Jesus Christ.

Third, the early Christians established small groups that met in homes for nurture and fellowship. Their entire existence focused on the small groups. It was in these small groups that they developed a sense of community. The "love feast" was a common practice at these house gatherings.

And fourth, the early Christians experienced persecution and arrest from religious and nonreligious people because their lives affected the economic practices of society and challenged the traditions of the religious leaders. These early Christian communities believed that they were dealing with a life and death issue. Being a witness to new life in Christ was dangerous and often resulted in the death of faithful followers.[6] A decision to become a "follower of the Way" often involved leaving family, job, friends, and security and sometimes resulted in death.

Based on these four essential concerns of the early church and what we know about the new emerging world, we can extract the following details about the first-century communities. The following section covers only the salient points pertaining to the mission of culturally relevant, Christ-focused congregations in the emerging new world.

1. *The primary task of the first-century Christians was to establish personal, Christian community in the midst of a hostile environment.* The biblical term for this personal community was *oikos*. In English it is translated as *household*. Paul and Silas used this term when they said, "Believe on the Lord Jesus, and you will be saved, you and your household" (Acts 16:31).

In *The Different Drum,* M. Scott Peck describes the kind of personal community that was at the heart of New Testament Christianity:

> If we are to use the word [*community*] meaningfully we must restrict it to a group of individuals who have learned how to communicate honestly with each other, whose relationships go deeper than their masks of composure, and who have developed some significant commitment to "rejoice together, mourn together," and to "delight in each other, make others' conditions our own."[7]

This kind of community seldom happens in groups of more than twenty people. Most of us limit our primary community to less than ten people.[8] From these significant others we find support, affirmation, accountability, and personal growth, or we experience our lives being destroyed by one of the members of our primary *oikos*. Each *oikos* is an integral part of the larger social structure called society. Every culture has been constructed this way.

The early Christian community took place in individual *oikoses* or small groups that routinely gathered in homes of Christians, not the institution that today we refer to as a church.

Jesus set the stage for these house groups, by spending much of his ministry in people's homes. He taught in homes, lived in someone's home, and served communion for the first time in someone's guest room. The disciples also lived in homes when they traveled.[9] Friends invited people to come see with their own eyes what God was doing. Conversions took place in their homes daily (I Cor. 14:24-25). Paul knew to go to people's homes to find the Christians to persecute— "But Saul was ravaging the church by entering house after house; dragging off both men and women, he committed them to prison" (Acts 8:3).

Over time, these house groups were networked together to form a local congregation.[10] The house groups gathered with other house groups to celebrate the "love feast" and to be taught by a traveling evangelist.[11]

The common meal (Holy Communion) was originally celebrated each time the house groups met. They would break bread, pass the cup, and be reminded that the church, the *ekklesia*, began at the Cross.[12]

2. *The task of these communities was to bring the kingdom of God (salvation or new life) to individuals.* The New Testament communities consisted of a people called out of the world and sent back into that world with a mission. They were commissioned to witness to the new life in Jesus Christ. Jesus said

"You will be my witnesses" (Acts 1:8). Over and over Acts portrays Christians as witnesses to this new life. The Holy Spirit was the power of the witness and the object was the new life found in Jesus Christ.[13] The only on-the-job training Jesus gave his disciples was door-to-door visitation. The early Christians told the world that God would go to any length to bring new life to us. Everything they did was geared toward that goal.[14]

Individuals, rather than a new world social order, were the objects of this new life. Concern for social justice occurred within the context of bringing new life to individuals.[15] Social justice was never addressed apart from a concern for bringing new life to the community of believers. God's relationship with Israel had already proven that neither morality nor salvation can be legislated.

Their mission was to equip people to live the new life, not to establish a church, or to enlarge the institution, or to add members to the roll. Membership in a church did not exist on the mission field. Daily participation in the Body of Christ was what mattered.

3. *These Christian communities were organized to nurture this new life and to equip individuals to bring new life to others.* Their identity was not in their buildings or programs but in the way that they brought new life to others. Intimate cell groups that moved from house to house were the heart of this movement. These "house churches" met daily for support and nurture and were considered as important as the weekly corporate worship. Christians held each other accountable (Acts 5:1-11). The early communities did not tolerate those who put personal profit before the common good.

Pastors equipped Christians to serve one another and to reach out to those not yet included in the fellowship. These communities understood their area of responsibility to be anyone they knew, beginning with the family, friends, and neighbors. As long as there was one individual who had not heard the good news, the mission of the church remained clear—to bring new life to everyone.

4. *"Jesus Christ is Lord" was the dominant theme of these early Christian communities.*[16] The proclamation of the life, death, and resurrection of Jesus Christ (notice, not his birth) set Christianity apart from all the other religions. The most primitive Christian creed was "in the name of the Lord Jesus" or "in the name of Jesus Christ." Remove this theme from the early church, and it resembled several other cults of that time.

Peter began the emphasis on the Lordship of Jesus Christ. When asked by Jesus who people thought he was, Peter answered: "You are the Messiah, the Son of the living God" (Matt. 16:16). Orthodox and nonorthodox disciples used this creed until around A.D. 254 when it became the source of controversy in Rome and Africa.[17]

The book of Acts carried this theme forward. Nineteen times Jesus is referred to in some way as "Christ the Lord."[18] This creedal formula is used in association with witnessing and receiving the Holy Spirit, healing, sources of pagan fear, Jewish jealousy, preaching, teaching, choosing a leader, exorcism, confession, worship, way to salvation, forgiveness of sins, requirements for Christian baptism, martyrdom, pagan attempts to use the name of Jesus, a badge of honor, and the kingdom of God. The last verse in Acts sums up the message and mission of the early church: "He lived there . . . proclaiming the kingdom of God and teaching about the Lord Jesus Christ with all boldness and without hindrance" (Acts 28:30-31).

This creed had more to do with how one felt than with what one knew. As this affirmation of faith was emphasized, the early Christians were turned outward to the world. Like Jesus, they began to live on behalf of others. And their numbers began to multiply.

These creeds were born out of a situation in which the Christian communities felt the need to describe their faith to non-Christians.

An important illustration of how the theological reflections finally
issued in fixed creeds is seen in the sermons in Acts. These contain an outline of the faith that was commonly held, *especially as
applied to missionary situations.*[19] (Italics are mine.)

The situation determined the style and form of the creed.
The only confession needed was the simple christological
affirmation "Jesus is Lord" or "Jesus is the Christ."[20] This
creed described the basic beliefs of the early followers of
Christ and was not an attempt to formulate a formal apolo-
getic. This creed contributed to the later developments of the
traditional creeds of Christianity.

Gnosticism was one of the earliest and most serious challenges to this early creed, and it was bitterly resisted because it
tried to develop an elaborate system of thought that removed
both God and Jesus Christ from the human dilemma. Salvation was knowledge rather than commitment to a Lord or
Christ. And this knowledge could be obtained from more
than one savior or illuminator. Disciples were encouraged to
turn inward and separate themselves from those lesser
humans who had not been enlightened. How one lived out
one's life ethically was not affected by this gnostic salvation.

The early Christian writers, primarily Paul, spent much of
their time refuting Gnosticism. The Pauline kergyma made
sure that the early church remained grounded in the simple
creedal formula, "Jesus Christ is Lord." According to Paul,

> The prophecies are fulfilled, and the new Age is inaugurated by
> the coming of Christ. He was born of the seed of David. He died
> according to the Scriptures, to deliver us out of the present evil
> age. He was Buried. He rose on the third day according to the
> Scriptures. He is exalted at the right hand of God, as Son of God
> and Lord of the quick and dead. He will come again as Judge and
> Savior of men.[21]

Even the earliest form of institutional summaries of the
basic tenets of Christianity affirmed the centrality of Christ.
Ignatius of Antioch wrote the following around A.D. 107:

Be deaf, therefore, whenever anyone speaks to you apart from Jesus Christ, who is of the stock of David, who is of Mary, who was truly born, ate and drank, was truly persecuted under Pontius Pilate, was truly crucified and died in the sight of beings of heaven, of earth and the underworld, who was also truly raised from the dead. . . .[22]

The so-called apostolic fathers agreed that all beliefs and practices of Christianity could be attributed to Christ himself. They taught that the ultimate source of doctrine came from the "Person, words and works of Jesus Christ in the context of the revelation of which He was the climax."[23] They even went so far as to say that Christ was the focal point of much of the Old Testament.

It was not until the third century that the binarian and trinitarian affirmations came into existence.[24] But these creeds, including the Nicene and Apostles' Creeds, are far too removed from early Christianity and too steeped in the situation of the institutional church to be of any help to us today. The third-century world was churched; ours is not.

Thus, the one distinctive element of the early Christian communities was "Jesus Christ is Lord." One primary assumption overshadowed everything else—everyone needed to become a follower of Jesus Christ. Belief in *Jesus Christ*—not the church, or the institution, or dogma—was the point of departure for life. Even receiving the Holy Spirit was accompanied by the creedal statement "Jesus is Lord." Jesus Christ was their reason for existence.

5. *The Holy Spirit empowered the witness of the early Christian communities and directed their actions.* If Jesus Christ was the point of departure for the early Christian communities' spiritual journey, the Holy Spirit was the power behind their proclamation. The Holy Spirit permeated everything these communities did. Once they affirmed that "Jesus Christ is Lord," the Holy Spirit took control.

The Holy Spirit provided the New Testament communities with the spiritual gifts needed to live an effective Christian life.[25] The Holy Spirit also directed the use of these gifts in such a way that when the group assembled, those who were not Christians realized that God was present (I Cor. 14:25).

The presence of the Holy Spirit not only enhanced the spiritual growth of Christ's followers but also increased the number of his followers as well. The Holy Spirit is usually presented in the New Testament in the future tense, always prodding the early church to move forward into new areas of ministry. Pentecost was the most notable of these events. As soon as the Spirit was poured out among the disciples, more people gave their lives to Christ (Acts 2:41, 47). The Holy Spirit pushed the disciples out of the safety of the upper room into the world. On the day of Pentecost, the Holy Spirit empowered the first outreach ministry of the church. This ministry was to bring people to proclaim that "Jesus Christ is Lord."

Peter's sermon on the day of Pentecost provides us the most primitive and basic response of the early Christians to the Holy Spirit. Jesus is the fulfillment of the Old Testament prophecy. He lived, died, was resurrected, and was exalted to the right hand of God. Jesus (not God) then poured forth the Holy Spirit. God made Jesus Christ both Lord and Christ; as a result, people must repent and be baptized in the name of Jesus Christ, receive forgiveness of their sins, and receive the Holy Spirit. The Lord added three thousand persons to their number. These believers enjoyed one another's company, remembered Christ as they ate together and prayed together, developed a common mission and went from house to house for community, had glad hearts, and spread the good news of God; "the Lord added to their number daily those who were receiving new life in Christ" (Acts 2:47). This is first-century Christianity. The world needs this kind of fellowship today.

6. *Prayer kept the early Christian communities focused on their mission to be witnesses of Jesus Christ.* "These all with one accord were continually devoting themselves to prayer." Taken in context, this verse shows the first century's single-minded passion for Jesus Christ. The subject of this *one mind* or *one accord*

53

was Jesus Christ. Jesus had just told them to be his witnesses to all the world (Acts 1:8). Then he left them alone to fend for themselves (Acts 1:10-11). One day later they returned to the upper room where they had been staying and "in one accord" prayed for the ability to endure the challenge. They prayed for strength to do what their Lord had asked them to do. They also wanted to add strength to their numbers, so they drew straws to replace Judas (Acts 16–26). They were preparing themselves for the journey to come. What a wonderful example for Christian churches today that sit in their modern upper rooms worrying about their survival instead of praying for the power to launch out on the journey with Christ.

7. *Leadership in the early communities was based on faithful service to Christ.* Leadership was defined as servanthood. Titles were avoided. Authority was based on how they lived rather than how much they knew. Trust and respect were earned through service to others.

Emphasis was placed on an individual's spiritual gifts.[26] Since no formal church structure existed, the early church encouraged people to discover their God-given gifts rather than fit into a particular need of the church. Pastors were to "equip the saints" for the purpose of building up the Body of Christ instead of fulfilling the person (Eph. 4:12).

At least twenty-five spiritual gifts were identified among the New Testament church. People were chosen for leadership on the evidence that they showed one or more of these gifts. No institutional credentials had developed.

Participants within the Christian communities held one another accountable.[27] When individuals received new life, they gave up their independence and individual rights for the benefit of the Body of Christ. Individuals found fulfillment as they served the common good. Each person was expected to find his or her place within the Body. Each person became a bearer of another's burden. The common good took precedence over individual rights.

8. *Early Christian communities were expected to stand on their own.* We have record of only one church receiving subsidy. On his second journey, Paul collected an offering for the church at Jerusalem. The irony is that the only church to receive subsidy is the same church that had earlier opposed Paul's method of evangelism. He was allowing people to experience the grace of God without submitting to circumcision. Some of the leaders of Jerusalem called Paul away from his ministry in Antioch and demanded that he stop preaching because he was abandoning a long-standing tradition. Although the matter reached a compromise settlement, it is significant that the Jerusalem church continued to decline in importance and strength because it clung to its tradition.[28]

Look at the contrast between a New Testament community and today's church.[29]

	New Testament Community	Today's Church
LOCATION	From house to house	Permanent place
SIZE	Small intimate, cells	Large, impersonal
DISCIPLESHIP	Word of mouth	Classes, notebooks
SUPPORT	Build up one another	See the pastor
LEADER'S TASK	Equip for ministry	Direct the program
PRAYER LIFE	Organized and daily	Limited and choice
PASTOR'S ROLE	Model discipleship	Preach good sermons
LAITY'S ROLE	Servanthood	Attendance
KEY WORDS	Go make disciples	Come grow with us
TEACHINGS	Apply Scriptures	Doctrinal beliefs
COMMITMENT	Increase the Kingdom	Enlarge the Church
PERCEPTION	Exercising God's gifts	Holding office in church
EVALUATION	How one serves	What one knows
STAFF	Servants from within	Professional
ACCOUNTABILITY	Everyone's role	No one's role

The Way Forward

Based on the example of the early Christian communities, the only way forward for congregations today is by turning outward to the world. Our leaders need an attitude adjustment. They need to focus the congregation on the world rather than themselves. Christians must shout to the world that Jesus Christ is Lord without being judgmental or forming value judgments regarding the worth of others. The greatest challenge of our time is to reclaim this essential evangelical part of faith without losing our passion for social justice or falling victim to the bigotry that often accompanies such a faith.

Are we able to affirm that Jesus Christ is Lord without becoming bigots? Is it possible for us to leave the christological question to God and at the same time passionately help people connect with God through Jesus Christ? If so, what does this community of faith look like today?

To be the church of Jesus Christ we must be willing to live in community, each one existing for the other. Is this possible in a world of radical individualism? Is this possible in a world of "live and let live"? If so, what does this corporate community look like today?

To be the church of Jesus Christ we must be willing to exist for the purpose of bringing new life to those who are not yet experiencing it. Can a society possessed with immediate gratification become such a community? If so, what does this corporate, Christ-focused community look like today?

To be the church of Jesus Christ we must be willing to spend our lives even unto death in order to turn society upside down and dismantle the sacred cows that bind us to a cultural religion. Can a self-centered culture, possessed with the fountain of youth, ever contemplate radical commitment? If so, what does this radical, sharing, corporate community look like today?

CHAPTER 5

The Demise of the Program-Based Church

....

Cells are not another ministry of the church;
cells are the church.
DALE GALLOWAY

Fringe people operate out of a set of paradigms that are totally for-
eign and radical to most established churches and church leaders.
But they work well. The congregations in which these fringe
people serve Christ develop caring networks and equipping
ministries in which laity care for one another and become
servants of Jesus Christ. Their congregations grow, not out of
a passion for growth, but because members take such incredible care of one another that laity invite their friends to join
them.

Chapters 5, 6, 7, and 8 examine the major paradigms out of
which these fringe people do ministry. Several such people are
mentioned in the following chapters in order to illustrate a paradigm. Keep in mind that "cookie-cutter" programs no longer
work. Ministries that work in one section of the country may
not work in another section. The emerging paradigms for the
twenty-first century are discovered when we find similar effective ministries occurring in several locations under different circumstances. The congregations in which these ministries are
found are referred to throughout the remaining chapters as
paradigm communities.

PARADIGM ONE

Small Group Ministries Are Replacing Programs

Two styles of ministry, each representing a side of the crack in history, are operating in North America at the moment. Program-based congregations are on the "what was" side of the crack; and small group-based congregations are on the "what is emerging" side.[1] The farther we move into the crack the less effective program-based congregations become and the more effective small group-based congregations become.

Many effective congregations are clinging to both sides of the crack, attempting to operate out of both styles of ministry. As the crack closes over the next fifteen years, those congregations caught in the middle, clinging to both sides of the crack, will experience serious frustration and decline. The small group-based congregations are on the fringe today. They will comprise the healthy denominations of the future.

Program-based congregations will decline for several reasons: (1) the sheer cost of planting and staffing the church; (2) the brokenness of our world requires a solid community life of fellowship which is found in only a few program-based congregations; (3) program-based churches have a way of isolating their members so far from those outside the church that evangelism is forced, and unnatural; (4) the 40 to 50 percent of inactives in the typical program-based church will continue to be siphoned away by the cell-based communities that reach out to them with caring ministries; (5) history has proven that program-based churches do not result in discipled, healthy, Christians.

The following two diagrams describe the basic difference between the two styles of ministry.

In the first model, the professional, ordained pastor performs the ministerial roles of caring for the congregation and recruiting new members. In the second model, the pastor is responsible for equipping the laity to minister to one another and take responsibility for their own ministry and

TRADITIONAL CARE MODEL

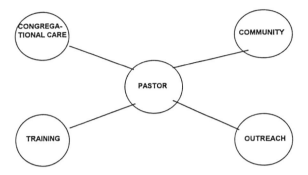

21ST CENTURY CARE MODEL

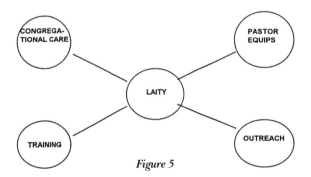

Figure 5

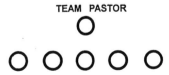

Figure 6

evangelism. In program-based congregations, pastors give and lay people receive. In small group-based congregations, the pastor equips and lay people give. The growth of congregations in the first model depends primarily on the population growth of the area. In the second model, congregational growth depends on the effectiveness of those equipping the laity and of the witness of the laity. The role of the pastor is to equip rather than to do; the role of laity is to be priest and theologian rather than spectator in the pew. In the first model, congregations can become cold and fragile and can easily overlook people. In the second model, congregations can never become cold or fragile. Ministry for both laity and clergy is helping people help others rather than holding an office in the church. This chapter is devoted to exploring the implications of laity and pastors making the paradigm shift from the program-based to the small group-based congregation.

1. *The transition from the program-based congregation to the small group-based congregation is the most fundamental paradigm shift in the history of North American Christianity.* In my first book, *The Church Growth Handbook,* I referred to worship as the first building block of congregational life.[2] That statement had held true for most of my ministry. It is no longer true today. In the crack in history, program-based churches are being replaced by a variety of effective small group-based communities.[3]

The one overshadowing practice of paradigm communities in America is their emphasis on small-group ministries. They build people, not churches. Their internal-care networks take incredibly good care of people. Newcomers are invited into small groups composed of people of similar background, need, or mission. The people become "bonded" to one another, instead of merely joining the church. Helping people discover a relationship with Christ and one another is the mission of these communities. Instead of focusing on programming and structural matters, leaders equip laity to become servants in caring networks. Acts 5:42 is often used as the basis for the development of these ministries. "Day after day, in the temple courts and from *house to house,* they never stopped teaching and proclaiming that Jesus is the Christ" (italics added).

Small group ministries are the primary ministry of paradigm communities. They are not one program among many; they are *the* program through which all ministry is accomplished. In small groups, people are supported, nurtured, discipled, and evangelized.

Paradigm communities are less concerned about "joining the church," "membership classes," or "transfer of your letter" than traditional churches. Such phrases assume that nonmembers are committed to the Christian faith, and that they respond positively to duty and obligation. Paradigm communities look for ways to bond people to the values and goals of the congregation. They know that new members tend to drop out of a church if they are not attached to a small group within two weeks of joining.[4] Bonding occurs best when individuals enter a significant relationship with a group. Since relationships are more important than members, they find their place in the congregation within the small group. Leaders know that just because a person goes through a membership class does not mean that they will remain a member.

Small group ministries perform almost all of the traditional roles played by the pastor in the program-based congregation. For example, when a person comes for counseling, the pastor evaluates his or her need, and while the person is still in the office, the pastor phones one of the leaders of an appropriate small group, and assigns the person to that group. This process may take forty-five minutes, and the pastor may never have to help that person again.

Evangelism and new member assimilation is done within the groups. Participants are encouraged to invite their friends to join them in their cell. Every first-time guest that registers is invited to attend a small group that same week.

New members are immediately assigned to a cell. It is not unusual for new members to know more about the congregation than long-time members who are not in a small group.

Four types of small groups are most prevalent among paradigm communities. Discipleship groups offer a high degree of accountability and reach about 10 percent of the people. Covenant groups offer short-term study groups and appeal to 30 to 40 percent of the people. Support and recovery groups reach about 60 percent of the people and require more training and preparation time. These groups usually meet weekly.

Small group ministries may be short term (Green Valley Evangelical Free Church near San Diego) or long term (New Hope Community Church in Portland, Oregon). Some congregations assign people to membership in a cell group (Willow Creek Church in Illinois); others allow the people to choose their own cell groups (New Hope Community Church).

Three small group models work well in both small and large congregations.

The most biblical and most effective small group ministry in North America is the *cell-based model*. This model is based on the New Testament model of the personal Christian communities that moved from one house to another. All of the basic spiritual needs of the people are met in the cells. These cells are not part of the paradigm community; they are the paradigm community. The cells make up the fundamental unit of the total paradigm community. Everything the community and staff do revolves around the cell ministries. *Everything* exists for the cells, is operated by the cells, and strengthens the life of the cells. Even evangelism is done through the cells as they are equipped and encouraged to multiply by starting new cells. Nothing competes with the life and ministry of these cells or those who lead them and those who train the leaders of the cell ministry. Cell-based communities celebrate and help individual members discover their spiritual gifts. This paradigm shift is so immense that it takes two or three generations of cell group multiplication before a true cell-based community emerges.

Cell members nurture one another and invite their unchurched friends to their group. When they grow beyond ten to fifteen people, they multiply by starting new cells. Each cell is always equipping one or more of the members to leave the group and train others. Multiplication before a cell reaches fifteen ensures that the cells do not become stagnated due to the same people sharing the same stories and needing the same type of care; that evangelism is central to the life of the cells. Cell ministries also ensure that Christians do not become isolated from unchurched people.

The finest example of the cell-based model in North America is the New Hope Community Church in Portland, Oregon, where Dale Galloway is the pastor.[5] The model is based on Acts 20:20: "I did not shrink from doing anything helpful, proclaiming the message to you and teaching you publicly and from house to house."

In the beginning, Pastor Galloway attempted to blend the cell ministry with the more traditional structures. He soon realized that he could not build a congregation around programs and build people at the same time. He did not have the time or the energy to do both. His first step was to inform his staff that their titles were changing from *Ministers* to *Zone Leaders*. Each staff person was to take responsibility for a particular zone of Portland, rather than a section of New Hope Church.

The city is divided into districts with a staff person over each district. Pastor Galloway personally trains each "lay pastor" who then takes responsibility for training the "cell leaders." Each week, people throughout Portland meet in small groups called TLC (tender loving care). Using this model, by 1992, New Hope Community Church was home to more than six thousand average worshipers; the average attendance at weekday cell meetings is over fifty-five hundred.

The cell-based concept of small group ministries is not one program among many programs with the congregation. Cells

63

are the basic Christian community. They are the way of life at New Hope. Everything revolves around the ministry of these groups. The pastors spend most of their time training lay pastors to train leaders of the cell groups.

Cells are kept between seven and fifteen people. They provide healing, nurture, support, and evangelism. They gather for a variety of reasons—consideration for common interests, mutual acquaintances, a missional interest, or simple geography. The cell groups at New Hope are divided into two tracts—support and nurture. Galloway says, "Support groups are the easiest groups to do, and anyone can do them."[6] The nurture groups are for healthy singles and families.

Each cell is encouraged to bring one new family to Christ every six months. Ninety percent of the lay pastors at New Hope Community Church lead a person to Christ every week. Eighty percent of the new growth comes from outside the church. Once a week all of the cell groups gather together to worship God.

About 50 percent of the membership at New Hope does not participate in the small group ministry. To make sure that they are nurtured, Galloway developed the "telecare ministry." Trained members of the congregation call the total membership every eight weeks to see if the church can be of help.[7]

The "meta church" is a very similar effective model of cell-based ministries. [8] The organizational principle for the meta model is the administrative advice Jethro gave Moses in the wilderness (Exod. 18). Carl George says, "Meta-math goes like this. If you can divide it by tens, it will carry tens of thousands; but if you divide it by hundreds, it will smother you with thousands."[9]

The caring network is divided into two basic levels of care. One level is "celebration" which is comprised of all the cells and congregations gathered for worship. The other level is cells of ten people. These are the basic organic unit of the congregation. Cells include care, study, prayer, accountability, and ministry responsibilities. An ideal cell consists of a cell pastor, team pastor, a seeker, an empty chair, growing disciples, one person equipped to handle people with special needs, a hospitality person, babysitter, and an apprentice pastor.

In most emerging cell-based congregations a third level exists in between the cells and celebration. These subcongregations are mid-sized groups larger than cells but smaller than celebration. They gather around a common purpose or need and provide relational avenues through which people find their way into the cells. These subcongregations are often foundational to the ministry in the traditional church, whereas they are elective in the meta model.

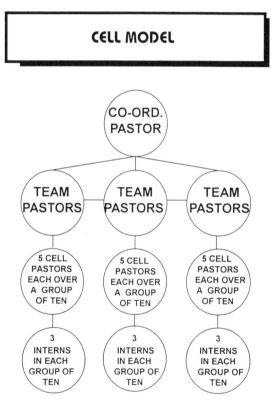

Figure 7

Each staff person (coordinating pastor) takes responsibility for fifty cells of ten people each. Each staff person then trains five lay people (team pastors) to take oversight of five cells of ten people each. These team pastors train a leader (cell pastor) for each of these five cells. Each cell has an apprentice that is being groomed to become a leader of a new cell of ten. When they exist, subcongregations are looked over by a congregational leader.

Once a month, cell pastors, team pastors, coordinating pastors, and congregational leaders gather for a three-fold purpose. The senior pastor communicates the vision for ministry to the collected leaders. The cell pastors and other leaders huddle in groups of five with their team pastor for prayer, sharing, and support. During these meetings, the participants are trained in both general ministry skills and specific ministry skills.

Because the meta model is organized for personal caring around tens rather than hundreds, it can be used in large or small congregations. It is large enough to minister and small enough to care. As the congregation grows, the organizational principles of the congregation do not have to change, which makes this model easier to break through the many natural barriers in church growth. A congregation can grow as large as it wishes while strengthening the caring ministries that people look for in a small congregation. For congregations where a Sunday school already exists, George recommends that the Sunday school be viewed as a "fishing tool to feed the cells."

Ginghamsburg United Methodist Church in Tipp City, Ohio, was a small, dying, rural church until it experienced tremendous growth in the last decade. Average worship attendance has grown from ninety to over twelve hundred in twelve years, although Ginghamsburg's official membership was only seven hundred in 1992. Such growth led to problems in assimilation, communication, nurture, and discipleship. Instead of ignoring these challenges, Ginghamsburg responded by developing the "Covenant Network," their name for the meta model. The ultimate purpose of the Covenant Network is to provide an environment of care and nurture in which the members of Christ's body are equipped to grow more Christ-like in character and servanthood. Nine hundred thirty adults are now involved in house groups.[10] The pastor, Mike Slaughter, describes the renewal of Ginghamsburg:

> I believe true renewal has more to do with theology than technique. It is an understanding of the church that is organic rather than organizational. Programs can be useful for getting people into the church, but they won't stay unless there is a deep movement of the spirit.[11]

Twice a month, the cell pastors of Ginghamsburg and their apprentices meet with their overseer, and the overseer meets with a coordinating pastor who is usually a staff person. This structure links the congregation together in a caring network that reduces the care-giving load on the staff and increases the amount of care giving throughout the congregation.

The success of cell-based ministries is dependent on three things: First, laity must be willing to release to the staff control of the day-to-day decisions of running the congregation and to agree to a number of predetermined ministerial roles for which they will take responsibility. Second, laity must be willing to receive pastoral care from other laity rather than always expecting it from the pastor. Third, pastors must be willing to spend the majority of their time training laity for ministry and then getting out of their way so they can actually be the ministers of the church. Both laity and pastors must give up control in very sacred areas. Laity must trust the pastor and staff to run the congregation, and pastors must trust laity to minister to one another. Dysfunctional pastors and laity that care more about controlling the institution than helping people find this model very threatening.

Many cell-based ministries have already matured to the point of developing cell groups for children and youth. These groups do not have teachers and pupils but leaders and members. They learn to pray for each other. The adult leaders seek to foster belonging as much as learning. The relational element is essential. "Life knowledge" as opposed to "head knowledge" is demonstrated. The children are encouraged to take responsibility for new children that enter the cell. Cells multiply when they reach twelve. Each cell trains a new cell leader, thus teaching children responsibility at a very early age.

Three aspects of the cell-based model make it a prime source for renewal in established, declining, or stagnant churches. First, it works in any size congregation. Size is not the issue. High quality care of people is the issue. If people are cared for in high quality ways, they respond by telling their friends. Thus, growth is an inevitable by-product of the small group ministries.

Second, the organizational structure of the congregation and the leadership skills of the pastor do not have to evolve as the congregation grows in size. As the program-based church grows, pastors soon learn that they must develop executive and administrative skills that often run counter to their interests. They discover that they can no longer work with people one-on-one, but have to work with selected groups of people. In time, pastors either keep the church at a small size so they can deal with people one-on-one, or they feel isolated or burned out. But cell-based congregations do not require a change in either the organizational structure or pastoral skills. The cells are the organization, the pastor always works closely with the groups of people, and the laity are not doomed to attend meetings.

Third, cell-based communities are not as expensive to operate as program-based congregations, so they have more money for ministry and missions. Program-based congregations need a program person for every hundred people in worship if the congregation is to take good care of the membership and reach out to the unchurched. Cell-based congregations only need one pastor or program person (including the pastor) for every three to five hundred people in worship.

According to Ralph Neighbor, a long-time student of cell-based ministries, the transition from a program-based church to a cell-based community takes from five to seven years.[12] Congregations wishing to make this transition find that at least six components are involved—radical redirection of the way pastors and laity understand and execute ministry, radical structural changes, the adoption of a new set of values, understanding the context in which the ministry is occurring, development of relational skills, belief and use of prayer, and the discovery of the role of the Holy Spirit in providing spiritual gifts.

Congregations making the necessary structural changes in the hope of becoming larger fail as cell-based congregations. The emphasis of the cell-based community is on smallness and on an effective caring network that builds strong Christians. These cell-based congregations are usually, but not always, on the conservative side, taking seriously the power of prayer and spiritual gifts. And in every case I have seen, the pastor is very much the spiritual authority for the congregation.

Poland United Methodist Church, located in Poland, Ohio, is a congregation attempting to make this transition with excellent results so far. When the process began in 1991, the church's average membership totaled seven hundred with only two hundred sixty-five in worship and one hundred in Sunday school. After a consultation with me, Pastor Dale Turner began the process slowly by handpicking twenty lay people who had the spiritual gifts of exhortation or prophecy. These twenty people agreed to spend forty-five minutes a week with the pastor for one year to be trained to become congregational lay leaders of a section of the congregation. (Although this violates one of the principles of the cell-based ministry, it is a place to begin; one year is too long to keep a person in training.) These twenty lay leaders are responsible for recruiting a team of two or three that they will train. Monthly gatherings of all team members are held for nurturing and fellowship.

A variety of ministry teams are also formed to provide avenues of service for people to use their various spiritual gifts. Some of these groups are visitation, computers, shut-in ministries, hospital visitation, telecare ministry, missions, Bible study leaders, and hosts at worship.

The telecare ministry assures that everyone in the membership absent from worship for three consecutive weeks receives a call. The pastor trains these callers to provide a caring message and collect any valuable information that will help in ministering to them.

Poland United Methodist Church has undergone a radical turnaround using this model. A long-term decline was reversed, and the congregation has grown in one year to three hundred in worship and one hundred seventy-five in Sunday school. (It will be interesting to see if the leaders of the United Methodist Church will give this pastor long enough to effect this transition before they move him. The itinerant system of appointing pastors on a short-term basis is a major deterrent to cell-based ministries.)

This paradigm shift may be the most difficult obstacle for clergy and laity to undertake. To make this shift pastors must be willing to become equippers rather than ministers, allow ministry to happen that they do not even know about, and trust laity to carry out the ministry. Making this transition changes everything we know about ministry. Laity must understand that ministry is serving others rather than holding office, be willing to give up control and turf, exist to serve those who have not yet been introduced to Jesus Christ, and allow the pastor to "run the church," while they do ministry.

The *ministry team model* offers a second model for effective small group ministry.[13] College Avenue Baptist Church in

San Diego, California, recruits people for a variety of ministry teams. Instead of recruiting people to hold office in the church, people are recruited to serve on ministry teams that help people. These teams vary according to the needs of the area.

A third effective small group ministry is the *support/recovery group model*. The people who come to these groups are viewed as prospects to hear the good news. These groups are led by trained laity from within the congregation, not by some outside group.

Such a ministry is offered at The Community Church of Joy (a Lutheran church) in Glendale, Arizona. Seventy percent of the people who attend their support and recovery groups come from outside their congregation. Thirty percent of these people end up joining the Church of Joy. Some of the groups they offer are Healing and Understanding; Alcoholics Anonymous; 3-D, Diet, Discipline & Discipleship, Divorce Recovery; Families Anonymous (for drug-related or behavioral problems); Healing the Hurts of the Past; Codependents Anonymous; Spouses of Handicaps; Job Seeker Support; Incest Survivors Anonymous; Domestic Violence Recovery; Parents of Adolescents; Moms Unlimited; Overcoming Sexual Addictions; and Caring for Aging Parents. Community Church of Joy is one of the largest congregations in North America.

A similar model is used for singles ministry in the Central Community Church in Wichita, Kansas. Each Tuesday night, hundreds of singles from across the city gather for a smorgasbord of small group experiences. Fifty percent of those attending are from outside the congregation. Some of the groups offered for singles are Al-Anon, His Loving Advocates (for families with a disabled member), Grief Support, Overcomers' Outreach, Abuse Recovery, Divorce Recovery, S.O.L.O (guidance for single mothers), Bible study, Stress and the Family, Volleyball, and ABC's of Weight Loss.

So many congregations in North America are interested in small group ministries that resources are springing up everywhere. North Star Strategies has been created to help program-based congregations make the difficult shift to becoming a cell-based congregation.[14] The *Cell Church Magazine* is now available to aid cell-based congregations.[15] In 1993, the Stephen Ministry experimented with a pilot project called "Pioneer Partners." The project is for congregations wishing to structure themselves around small group ministries. Ralph Neighbor's book *Where Do We Go from Here?*[16] Carl George's book *Prepare Your Church for the Future,* and Dale Galloway's book *20/20 Vision* are sources for further reading on the phenomenon of cell-based congregations.

All of these models have great potential: they replace the issue of growth with an emphasis on a caring system for individuals; they offer an organizational model that can be used in any size congregation; they allow one pastor to effectively shepherd more than one hundred people (the norm for growing traditional churches); they overcome the clergy shortage of the future; they replace the emphasis on the preaching ability of the pastor with an emphasis on the caring ability of the congregation; they are one of the best ways to break a thousand in worship—the most difficult growth barrier. These models will do well in an age of shrinking dollars and clergy, alienated laity, and a hostile environment.

Centering a congregation's ministry around small groups causes fundamental changes throughout the congregation. Consider the following.

2. *The domestication and marginalization of the laity is over.* For decades, clergy have dominated the life of our congregations. Laity have been treated like house pets who spend most of their time, energy, and dollars doing housekeeping chores within and around the church grounds. But paradigm communities are rediscovering the biblical role of the laity. The priesthood of the believer is taking the place of the institutionally oriented professional clergy. The care and nurture of

the congregation is accomplished through the laity. The purpose of the paid shepherd is to equip and lead the laity into society to bring new life to others.

The Bible teaches that every Christian is a priest of God and thereby responsible for the ministry of reconciliation (I Pet. 2:1-5). No biblical precedent exists for the term *minister* to be reserved for the clergy. Every Christian is called by God to be a minister.

Jürgen Moltmann clearly states the role of the laity in the renewal of Christianity:

> The renewal of the church finally depends on what happens at the grass-roots level. And renewal at this level awaits, it seems to me, on the conscious reclaiming of the gifts of the Spirit on the part of the laity. These gifts, which in the New Testament are always identified as signs of the coming Kingdom of God, are given to the whole people of God for ministry, for diakonia.[17]

3. *Equipped laity replace ordained clergy.* Paradigm communities are redefining the role of ordained clergy. Clergy are no longer considered "set apart" due to ordination. Pastors are sought with the ability and passion to share their faith with others regardless of their academic credentials.[18] Emphasis on ordination is replaced with an emphasis on the ministry of all believers. Clergy are expected to work toward the expansion of the kingdom of God rather than maintaining what already exists. Career clergy will remain frustrated because their congregations and their personal level of fulfillment will continue to decline. The day is over when ordained clergy can feel superior to nonordained persons.

I had an eye-opening experience while serving on my denomination's restructuring committee. The committee, made up equally of laity and clergy, concluded that a resident CEO was needed to run the conference due to the frequent absence of the bishop. The laity wanted this position to be filled by a layperson so that denominational leaders could not fill it with a clergy person who had gotten in trouble or who was being rewarded for reasons other than ability. It was clear to the laity that a "clergy union" existed and that the need of the clergy was taking precedence over the need of the local congregations.

4. *Laity are encouraged to discover their spiritual gifts rather than hold various offices in the church.*[19] Most churches ask new members to fit into predetermined offices and roles that benefit the institutional church. Paradigm communities take a different approach to lay ministry. Spiritual inventory tests are provided to help laity discover their basic passion for ministry. They are encouraged to develop their ministry around one or two of their strongest gifts instead of fitting into a particular ministry that the church requires. The role of staff and experienced laity is "to equip the saints" to do the work of ministry that fits his or her gifts.[20] In these communities, laity visit hospitals, share in crises ministries, and do many of the functions traditionally done by clergy.

Building up the Body of Christ is the goal of spiritual gifts, not meeting the needs of the participants. Their needs are met as they find their God-given place in the Body of Christ. Instead of rotating their service around various offices in the church, participants are encouraged to develop their ministry in one or two areas. Laity develop long-term expertise in a particular area which they can use to train others who have their same gift, but no experience. Burnout is minimized because the participants are doing what they enjoy and do well.

Colonial Hills, the church I served Christ in for twenty-four years, instituted the spiritual gifts inventory in 1992. We offered two levels of inventory tests. All new members were given the short form when they joined, and every member was given the opportunity to take the inventory during worship and in the weekly newsletter. Members who wanted to learn more about their place in God's world were encouraged to take the longer form. Based on their test results and what we already knew about them, selected members were invited to have an hour consultation with one of the pastors to determine their ministry on behalf of the Body of Christ. In the first three months, we experienced an explosion of new leadership.

5. *Laity are the effective theologians on a mission field.* The laity are in the spiritual trenches every day. Growing communities are equipping and consecrating laity to do ministry in the workplace rather than nominating them to serve within the organizational structure of a congregation.[21] Laity rub shoulders with more unchurched people in one week than many pastors do in a year. They need to be theologians who can answer the questions that people are asking today: Who is God? What is God like? How do I find God? What is salvation? How do I pray? How do I find meaning and purpose for my life?

6. *Inviting people is the first priority of Christians on a mission field.* Paradigm communities exist to bring new life to others so that they can be equipped to go back out into the world to bring new life to others. On a mission field Christians gather to worship in order to spread the good news. Instead of waiting for people to come to them, laity are equipped to invite people to small home groups or to worship. Concern for privacy is considered, but it is not nearly as important as the passion to share with others the good news of new life.

Two personal experiences best describe their passion for evangelism. During a consultation with a dying congregation, a discussion ensued about the possibility of the congregation operating a television ministry. Their primary concern was clear: Will it pay for itself? During a consultation in a paradigm community, the same discussion had a different ending. Their concern was quite different: How many people will a television ministry win to Jesus Christ?

The goal of ministry for paradigm communities is never simply to meet people's needs. Paradigm communities meet people's needs to establish a relationship with them that allows the congregation access into their lives. On a mission field everything is done through the eyes of evangelism. Everything paradigm communities do is based on two objectives: inviting people into the faith, and discipling those who respond. These communities establish relationships with people to hold them long enough for them to discover new life in Christ. A weekday children's ministry that meets the needs of working parents is great, but any organization can do that. Weekday child care is provided to establish an entry point into the lives of the children and their parents and then introduce them to God. Congregations involved in social justice ministry, do so for the purpose of bringing the news of Jesus Christ to those whose lives are touched by the changes made in the system. Soup kitchens and shelters for the homeless are for the purpose of establishing relationships from which to share the good news of new life. Hard-core community organizing is done not to change the system as much as to change people who will change the system. Bazaars are for the purpose of getting names and addresses of those who attend, not raising money. The goal is to move people from self to God, from self to others, from self to the Body of Christ. To accomplish this transformation today we must first establish a relationship with the unchurched.

7. *Ministry is defined as servanthood rather than holding office.* Two years after Colonial Hills restructured in 1986 to eliminate most of the standing committees and equip more laity in ministry, a long-term member angrily asked me, "How are we going to identify new leaders when we have so few meetings?" [22] I told him that I did not understand his question. He responded, "If we don't have meetings to see how faithfully people attend or how well they run a meeting, how are we going to select new leadership?" This man grew up in an age of male-dominated bureaucracies. To him, ministry was going to meetings and leadership was conducting a meeting. I replied, "Now we choose leaders on the basis of how well they serve others." It never dawned on him that leaders could be selected on the basis of servanthood.

Today, leaders are defined as those who serve rather than those who run the church. Respect and authority come from servanthood, not credentials. Titles and status are not important. Younger adults no longer are content going to meetings.

PARADIGM TWO

Pastors Equip Persons Rather Than Do Ministry

Dysfunctional and/or career-oriented pastors may be threatened by small group-based models for ministry. Pastors that have a need to be needed in order to find validation for their ministry will have a hard time giving up control of the actual ministry to the congregation. Pastors who need to keep the laity dependent on them will avoid these forms of ministry. Pastors who entered the ministry to find a safe, warm environment will find these ministries too challenging for their spiritual cocoons. Pastors who are interested only in maintaining the status quo will not do well with small group-based ministry.

In their book *Rekindling the Flame* Willimon and Wilson make this valuable observation: "The clergy must be convinced that the churches mission is more important than their needs."[23] Making this decision is the key to the success of small group-based ministries.

1. *The pastor's role is primarily to teach and equip laity for ministry in the world, not to perform ministry on behalf of the church.* When a layperson tells Randy Pope, the pastor of Perimeter Church of Greater Atlanta, that he or she is not able to carry out a ministry, Randy tells them "then I have failed you. I have not equipped you."

Equipping pastors have a vision and train people to bring about that vision. People join in the ministry because they are inspired by that vision and are anxious for the vision to become a reality. When equipped, they make the vision a reality. The equipping pastor does very little ministry.

Instead, the equipping pastor steps aside and encourages the laity to be the ministers of the congregation.

Do not confuse equippers with enablers. Enablers do not have a vision of their own. They help a congregation go only where it wants to go. Aaron was an enabler and the result of his efforts was a golden calf (Exod. 32). Equippers have a vision and often take the congregation where it would not go on its own. Moses was an equipper.

Equipping is a fundamental change for professional clergy. Most have been trained to enable and to perform ministry for the congregation. Becoming an equipper is difficult, but those clergy who do not make this change will continue to experience burnout, stress, confusion, and lack of success in helping people develop spiritually.

The major role of clergy in cell-based ministry is developing lay pastors to carry out the primary work of ministry both in and out of the community.[24] These lay pastors commit a specific amount of time each week to ministry once they are trained. They function as paid staff with the exception of the time they can invest. The pastor spends the vast majority of time training and supporting these people. They in turn take care of the congregation. In the other small group-based models pastors and staff spend most of their time establishing small groups and equipping laity to run them.

2. *Pastorates average twenty to thirty years in the twenty-first century.* Paradigm communities are experiencing long pastoral tenures followed by a carefully chosen successor. Small group ministries that include trained, lay pastors work best when continuity among all staff is maintained as long as possible.[25] Remember, this model is based on relationships rather than program. As long as a match between pastor and congregation continues, the pastor stays. The longer the pastorate the more likely a congregation is to be strong and growing.

Ten additional factors make longer pastorates more effective: (1) Significant ministry often occurs after the sixth or seventh year. (2) The honeymoon is over at eighteen months;

78

conflict is normal. (3) The first four years are spent forming relationships within the congregation. (4) Around the third or fourth year, active members who care more about control than ministry begin to realize the pastor is becoming one of the congregation and threatens their power base. (5) During the sixth year, either an engagement occurs or the pastor is moved. (6) If the engagement occurs, a marriage takes place the seventh year and the pastor and the people become one. (7) Baby boomers join personalities or groups rather than organizations. After four or five years, they transfer their allegiance from the pastor or group to the local congregation. When pastors move often, young adults move also because they have not had time to identify with the congregation as a whole. (8) Strategic planning is easier to achieve when pastors move no more than once every ten years. Laity are hesitant to make serious plans for the future because they know the tenure of the pastor is so tenuous. This is especially true with small churches. (9) Pastors and congregations need time for seeds to germinate and to learn from their mistakes. (10) Pastors who move often never learn from their mistakes.

Succession is one of the most important aspects of a senior pastor's ministry in the twenty-first century. Senior pastors with more than five hundred in worship are spiritual CEOs and need to have major input into the selection of their successors. According to *Fortune* magazine, picking a successor is one of the three responsibilities of a CEO.[26]

3. *Well-trained, bivocational, nonordained persons replace ordained clergy.* It is not unusual in established denominations for a full-time ordained clergy to pastor a congregation of seventy-five to ninety members. In most cases these congregations are dying. However, studies show that well-trained lay pastors can often strengthen small congregations where ordained clergy cannot.[27] These persons are usually more productive for the following reasons: (1) The congregation is often immobilized by the cultural shock experienced when an ordained pastor right out of seminary comes to a small or

rural congregation. (2) Nonordained persons are often better care-givers because they are more in tune with the needs of laity. (3) Nonordained persons tend to stay in one place longer because they are not as career oriented as ordained persons. (4) Nonordained persons tend to be more conservative than ordained clergy which fits the theological stance of most small congregations. (5) Small congregations are more likely to afford a nonordained person instead of having to depend on any kind of subsidy.

Lyle Schaller suggests that congregations with twenty-five members or less should be lay led, congregations with twenty-five to seventy-five members should be led by bivocational laity, and congregations with seventy-five to one hundred fifty should be led by a bivocational team.[28]

Conclusion

The twenty-first century will be an exciting time for ministry. Pastors who are secure enough to risk and venture into uncharted waters will do well. They will create a variety of new ministries that reach a variety of new needs and hurts. Their ministry will focus on the laity and their role in passing on to society the good news. And they will turn them loose to effectively minister in the world, not at church.

These venturesome pastors will make another incredible change in ministry. They will develop indigenous worship that celebrates what God has done rather than promote Anglican worship which smacks of a funeral dirge and begs God to "charge the spectators' batteries." Chapter 6 is about this new paradigm in worship.

CHAPTER 6

A Reformation
in Worship

....

We are in the second stage of the Reformation.[1]
JACK HAYFORD

*If small group ministries are the most fundamental paradigm shift
in the history of North American Christianity, the shift in the style of
worship is the most obvious and devisive.* This divisiveness is over
the style of worship rather than doctrine or theology. Congregations and pastors are more likely to split and form new relationships over worship styles than theology. Few changes will
affect the future of a congregation more than those made in
worship.

If your congregation still worships through long liturgies
and stately hymns of earlier generations, the odds are your
congregation is declining. If it is growing, it is probably due
to a growth in the population. Paradigm communities grow
in any climate because of their style of worship.

PARADIGM ONE
Effective Worship Is Culturally Relevant

Effective worship today grows out of the culture of the
area. The style and form is comfortable to those attending
worship from the non-Christian world.[2] The message remains
the same, but the package in which the message is conveyed
is conditioned by the culture of the times. Paradigm commu-

81

nities conform the package of worship without compromising the content of the message.

1. *Paradigm communities focus worship on God.*[3] Most unchurched people today are looking for answers to spiritual questions. Their questions may not be couched in biblical terminology, but they are biblical nonetheless. They are asking intense questions about the meaning of life. Paradigm communities are convinced, beyond any doubt, that God is the answer to these questions. For these congregations, worship is for the purpose of adoring and praising God for who God is and what God can do in our lives. Worship is vertical. Worship emphasizes the mystery and majesty of God.[4]

On the surface, this paradigm hardly seems to represent a major shift in thought or action. Most church members say that worship is about God. But their actions suggest that they "come to church" to worship something other than God. Two examples make the point.

In a northeast section of the United States, three churches of the same denomination are located on three of the four corners of the same intersection. One congregation is the result of a denominational merger twenty-five years earlier. Another is the original church of the larger of the two merging denominations. The third church is the result of another merger some one hundred thirty years earlier. The combined worship of all three churches is less than one hundred people. Each church exists on a piece of land not much bigger than a postage stamp, leaving no place for parking or weekday ministries. All of the churches are struggling to survive and keep their facilities maintained. The combined facilities are worth around two million dollars. Two of the churches are subsidized by the denomination. None of the churches are willing to talk with the others about becoming one congregation. Together, they could probably conduct a valuable ministry. But they will not consider giving up their property.

At one congregation in the Midwest, the average attendance was less than one hundred. One year earlier, the congregation started a contemporary worship in hope of reaching younger people. During the year, attendance almost doubled. The congregation should have been pleased. Instead the congregation was split over the success of the new service. During the short lifespan of the second service, most of the children and youth, along with many of the older members, had gravitated to the new service along with many new young people. I heard one of the long-time members express her anger: "We're no longer able to see all our friends." Another angry member chimed in, "I miss seeing the children. Why do we have to have two services?" Before long, all of the angry members were voicing the same self-centered view of worship. They came to church to see their friends and to be with the children. It was as if the children came to church for their benefit. No one remembered that before the new form of worship, the children did not want to attend worship at all.

Worship is about God—not us, our friends, or the children we no longer have at home. Paradigm communities fellowship with the spiritual family at times other than worship. Horizontal relationships with friends occur in small group ministries. Worship is the time when the small fellowship groups come together to adore God. It is the Body of Christ honoring God that gives life to the worship service. Paradigm communities do not try to cram celebration, nurture, meditation, and fellowship into one hour on Sunday morning.

2. *Celebration of God is the heart of worship.* The 1990s have given us little to celebrate. Bad news flows in on a regular basis. Hope is needed in large doses today.

The generation following the baby boomer is one of the most cynical generations in American history. They do not like boomers. They know that their generation will not have it nearly as good as the boomers did. They know that the generations before them have not taken care of the planet Earth.

They see very little hope in their future. I call them the clean-up generation.[5] They will have to clean up the mess left over from the party of the 1980s. They require large doses of joy and celebration.

The clean-up generation does not want to be reverent or quiet during worship. Paradigm communities encourage clapping and consider it a form of the "Amen" of revival days, or the "right on" tradition in African-American congregations. They avoid signs like "Enter in Silence: Worship in Progress." They encourage meditation in the small home groups instead of during worship.

3. *Music is the major vehicle for celebration and communication.* Music is an integral part of life for people under forty-five years of age. It is the vehicle through which most unchurched people experience worship. Whereas my generation was not allowed to listen to music while we studied, today people study, jog, work, sleep, and meditate to music. Few movies can make a profit without a solid sound track.

The type of music that reaches people comes out of their culture. Culturally relevant music can be discovered by determining what radio stations most of your worship guests (not members) listen to. This can be achieved by taking 30 seconds in worship to have your guests write down the two stations they listen to the most, or by asking radio stations for their ratings broken down by age brackets. Every survey will show that "soft rock" is the music of the majority of unchurched people in America. Only four percent of the records sold in the United States are classical.[6]

Symphony orchestras all over North America are experiencing what happens to organizations that fail to realize the fundamental change in North America's musical tastes. The whole symphonic enterprise—the repertoire, the ambiance, the culture—does not connect with a large enough or young enough audience to give much hope for the long term. Classical music was rooted in the native folk music of the time. That world is gone. Few if any symphonies in North America will survive the next few decades without major changes that include introducing more pop and rock music.

> If you take time to study the impact of music on our culture, you will find that the music of the baby boomer generation (predominantly rock 'n' roll) is likely to dominate the culture of our society well into the next century. Even our children are very comfortable with our musical tastes and identify easily with them.[7]

John Bisagno, pastor of First Baptist Church in Houston, Texas, minces no words when he describes the debilitating effects that classical music has on worship in most settings:

> Long-haired music, funeral-dirge anthems, and stiff-collared song leaders will kill the church faster than anything in the world. Let's set the record straight for a minute. There are no great vibrant, soul-winning churches reaching great numbers of people, baptizing hundreds of converts, reaching masses that have stiff music, seven-fold amens, and a steady diet of classical anthems. None. That's not a few. That's none, none, none.[8]

The rise of contemporary music has been aided by the services of organizations such as Christian Copyright Licensing, Inc., which for a fee, gives permission for congregations to print thousands of songs or to use overhead transparencies or slides during worship.[9]

4. *Music is **the** ritual of our time.* Music is replacing the written liturgy with which many Christians grew up. Music achieves the same results once accomplished by responsive readings, creeds, psalters, and corporate prayers. It is the vehicle or conduit through which the message is conveyed. It is a setting in which Christians praise and adore God. Background music has its place; preludes and postludes may be played as worshipers enter and exit the church.[10]

It is not unusual for music to comprise 40 percent of worship in paradigm communities.[11] Music permeates every part of the service. No more than three or four seconds go by without music (except during the sermon). Prayer time is supported by background music. Communion is received in the midst of congregational singing. Even parts of the sermon may have some form of musical accompaniment.

Worship is not the place to teach music appreciation. Paradigm communities ask one question when choosing music: Does it bring people closer to God? The only acceptable music is that which conveys the message of new life. Music is never the message itself, no matter how well it is presented. No form is inherently better than another. Music is good if it conveys the gospel; it is bad if it does not.

Spiritual giants such as Martin Luther and Charles Wesley showed us the importance of culturally relevant music. They met the needs of the culture of their day by taking the tunes out of bars, putting words to them, and using the songs in worship. They accommodated the needs of people in order to reach them with the message that would eventually change their lives. They did not conform the message, just the package.

Synthesizer, drums, flute, electric guitar, tambourine, bass, and piano are the basic instruments of today. A culturally relevant worship center must include a quality sound system with these instruments, microphones, monitors, a sound engineer, and good acoustics, as well as lighting, and large projection screens. All of the senses must be stimulated if the gospel is to get through to people reared on electronics.

Hymnals are often discarded or supplemented with praise choruses that reflect contemporary tastes in music. The words to the songs are displayed on a large, elevated screen. People look up and around instead of burying their faces in a hymnal or looking down at their feet.

One study of Southern Baptist churches revealed that the quality of the contemporary music is one of the strongest factors in church growth, regardless of size. Ninety percent of the large congregations rated the quality of their music as excellent. Sixty-five percent of the smaller growing congregations rated the quality of the music as excellent or good. Only 37 percent of small churches at a plateau and 35 percent of declining churches rated their music as excellent.[12]

Choirs are becoming optional and are often replaced by ensemble leadership groups. Solos, groups, praise teams (consisting of three or more people singing close harmony), instrumentalists, choruses, and medleys provide a wide range of choices and also involve a variety of people in small groups. The larger the congregation, the more small musical groups are formed to supplement or replace the traditional choirs.

Worship teams are developed in paradigm congregations. These teams consist of the pastors, choir directors, drama teams, testimonials, prayer groups, ushers, praise teams, soloists, and so forth. When choirs are present they form a part of the worship team. They assist in leading worship the entire time they are present, not just when they sing. Their presence sets a tone and setting. Their prayers are part of the power. Word and song combine to paint a powerful picture for the unchurched generation.

The Community Church of Joy in Glendale, Arizona, has grown from fewer than one hundred in worship to more than twenty-five hundred in the decade since a new pastor introduced the church to contemporary music. This paradigm community has an organ that is used only for weddings.

Caution: Changing the music habits of declining or stagnant congregations is proving to be a major cause of conflict. Shepherd of the Hills Church in Los Angeles switched to contemporary music, eliminated hymnals, and did not include an organ in its new sanctuary. The results were two-fold: the average age of the congregation dropped from thirty-six to twenty-seven, but many of the older members complained that the music was too loud and they missed the old hymns played on the organ. Recently, a small electronic organ was purchased to be used for solemn background music during prayers.[13]

The source of the conflict comes primarily from trained musicians who often find these concepts repugnant and resist any change in the style of music. Church musicians do more to hinder congregations from sharing new life than any other staff members. Many are more interested in music appreciation than in helping people find new life. They are musicians first, and worship leaders second. Their love for music rivals their love for Christ. Making disciples is not as important as making good music. It is time we recognize this problem and deal with it accordingly.

It was necessary to change choir directors when Colonial Hills made the transition from traditional to contemporary worship in 1989. We needed more than just a choir director—we needed a worship leader, someone who could teach Christianity to the choirs and congregation through the music. The change cost us half of the existing choir and a considerable amount of conflict from longtime church members who preferred classical music over other kinds of music. The choirs became much younger, larger, and more creative than ever before. More important, many more choir members now understand and live what they sing.

5. *Two styles of worship are needed in congregations that have reached their plateaus or are declining.* Aging congregations cannot be expected to give up a style of worship that fits their culture in order to reach the younger generations. Neither is it fair to ask the younger generations to worship in the culture of the older generation. It is much easier to start a separate and distinct worship service.

Colonial Hills experienced two other changes when we shifted to contemporary music: Worship attendance moved dramatically upward from a two-year plateau, and the older generation complained that the music was too loud and that they missed the traditional elements such as Apostles' Creed and Doxology. They felt that no one in the church cared about them anymore. As a result, we made one service traditional and solemn to satisfy the wants of the older generation.

Established congregations must find ways to validate the cultural needs of the older generation while not forgetting that the future of their congregation depends on the younger generation.

Congregations wishing to begin a culturally relevant service can ask the membership to buy into the concept at any one of three levels. First level: They simply give permission for the service to be started. They neither participate nor condemn the new service. Second level: Money is allocated in the budget for the purpose of starting and advertising the service but they neither attend nor promote it. Third level: Members actively participate in promoting and helping the service become successful.

6. *Entertainment is an integral part of contemporary evangelism.* In 1987, a Lutheran congregation in Arizona began what they call entertainment evangelism. They replaced their sedate liturgical traditions for contemporary music, drama, and upbeat sermons. Since then, the congregation has grown from eighty-seven members to six thousand members. "We're trying to take seriously why people don't come to church," said Assistant Pastor Timothy Wright, who believes that today's baby boomers are turned off by the rote liturgy and classical organ music typically incorporated in most Lutheran worship services.[14]

One of the questions pastors ask me the most is, Where do we draw the line between proclamation and entertainment? I wonder where people get the idea that worship must be boring to have integrity. Most churches have so far to go before they even get near crossing over the line between entertainment and proclamation that they should be asking, What can we do to make our churches less boring and more relevant? Worship can have integrity without being boring.

When the decision was made in 1989 to make worship at Colonial Hills as contemporary as possible, we wanted to make sure that the music had theological integrity. Our only concern with contemporary Christian music was that some of it conveyed horrible theology. We solved the theological issue by choosing choruses that put biblical words to music. The only criticism anyone can make is that they do not like the type of music.

Many paradigm communities use music and drama as a major form of reaching out to the unchurched. Quality Christian music, combined with drama, reaches the emotions of most young adults better than anything else. They can convey in very powerful ways what the spoken word cannot. Willow Creek Community Church, outside of Chicago, has used drama since its beginning. Each service includes a five- to ten-minute drama that sets the stage for the message by raising the questions dealt with in the message.[15]

In San Antonio, Texas, Trinity Baptist Church uses *The Living Christmas Tree* as a method of reaching the unchurched. Members are given free tickets to give to their friends. The performances span several days and each performance is filled to capacity. The message that comes through to the people is biblical and inspiring.

Perimeter Church of Greater Atlanta sold three thousand tickets to the musical *Back in Time*. The songs of the sixties were analyzed by looking at the needs, hurts, and motivations in the music. At the end of the presentation, the pastor discussed how Jesus was the answer to the needs of the people of the sixties. Another church includes free tickets to its concert series in the new members' packets and encourages them to give the tickets to their unchurched friends.

7. *Culturally relevant music is essential in a nonwhite world.* Congregations that provide contemporary music attract people of all backgrounds. The Euro-centric stodginess that surrounds so much of the classical scene was perpetuated since the Reformation in order to keep out the riffraff. As long as classical music prevails in worship, the rank and file of the United States, most of whom will be of ethnic minorities by the middle of the twenty-first century, will continue to stay away from churches.

8. *Effective preaching takes practice, makes a passionate appeal to emotion more than fact, and paints a visual picture of the subject.* People respond to preaching today through their emotion; then they justify their decision with facts (how faith meets their needs). In order for people to hear what is being said (fact or content), they must first experience the speaker's energy. How one behaves while preaching is as important as what one says. Too many notes, large lecterns, and repeated glances at the floor are three of the best ways to lose a congregation's interest.[16]

Browse through any secular bookstore and notice the size of the self-help section. "How-to books" sell to the masses; theoretical books do not. The message must be useful throughout the week. Some communities encourage people to write down the major points of the sermon and refer to them during the week. Others provide an outline of the sermon with blanks for people to fill in during the sermon. Some pastors read the scripture and then review one or two points that they want the people to take home with them before they start the sermon.

9. *Worship is casual.* Suits and ties are no longer an essential part of worship for the "jeans generation." More and more communities have "jean month" when even the staff wear jeans. Some have services where shorts or jeans are the norm all year. Chancel areas are more friendly when they do not have a rail separating the worship leaders from the worship participants. Choirs may even sit unrobed in the congregation. Robert Schuller's drive-in worship was one of the early forms of casual worship.

One year when Christmas Day was also a Sunday, a congregation advertised Christmas Sunday as "Come as you are" Sunday to the whole community. The service was well attended. One family bought matching pajamas. The tuba player sat on the stage (some call it the chancel area) in shorts and thongs. The pastor preached in a turtle neck sweater. Most people said it was one of the most meaningful services they ever experienced.

PARADIGM TWO
Buildings Are Not Important

People who worship God do not become attached to buildings or locations. Instead, they are free to discover creative ways to reach the unchurched. The fringe communities are developing a variety of ministries not dependent on location or facilities.

Many congregations cannot continue to do effective ministry in their present location. Either they need to relocate, close, or develop satellite ministries. For this reason, most of the strong, large paradigm communities have not been started yet or have been started within the last twenty years. Ask yourself this question: If I were choosing a location for the congregation where I serve Christ, would I put it where it is today? If your answer is no, your congregation is a candidate for relocation or satellite ministries.[17]

1. *Multiple-site campuses are becoming common.* These experiments are called satellites, or geographically expanded (or perimeter) parish churches.[18] They operate on the hub-and-spoke concept with one central congregation and many branch congregations.[19]

Multiple-site congregations are becoming common for several reasons: (1) Overhead costs are reduced; (2) people are more focused on God than on buildings or sacred furniture or rooms; (3) congregations located on postage stamp properties, unable to relocate due to the cost, can still grow; (4) creative congregations can have a variety of ministries in a variety of locations; (5) congregations can do ministries that are conflicting in nature such as half-way houses and weekday child care.

One of the most creative models for small congregations is occurring in the six-year-old Cornerstone Mennonite Church in the Shenandoah Valley of Virginia. Cornerstone has developed four satellite congregations located in small, rural towns surrounding Harrisonburg where most congregations are declining. All four congregations are listed in local phone book under one name. They are led by "branch pastors" from within each congregation who are trained at the Bible College of the mother congregation. Each congregation has its own budget that is administered from a central organization. According to the administrative pastor, Cornerstone is attempting to "move away from buildings controlling our growth to relationships controlling our growth."[20] They do not use the words *church* or *Mennonite* in their advertising. Many of the people who join have had bad experiences in churches that failed to provide them with a caring network.

The mother congregation planted the satellites by sending fifty members out to a targeted location to begin each new congregation. In 1992, these four satellite communities had a total summer average worship of over one thousand with the mother congregation averaging around four hundred fifty.

Another creative model began in 1977 in the Perimeter Church of Greater Atlanta.[21] Their vision is to plant a congregation that will have eventually one hundred locations. By 1992, ten congregations have been established around the perimeter of Atlanta. New congregations are established about every three years. Some of the congregations are as far away as ten miles in surrounding suburbs. The pastors are all associated with the main congregation, but the congregations remain autonomous. Each congregation contributes 5 percent of its total income to what is now Perimeter Church Ministries for the purpose of planting other congregations.

The organizing principle behind satellite ministries is effective ministry, not doctrinal sameness. Paradigm communities seem to be defined more by their style of ministry than by their doctrine. How they minister is more important than what they teach. Before the crack of history, people chose to worship with people of "like faith." Today, people choose to worship with people of "like ministry." It is very possible that new denominations will emerge from experiments such as this.

93

2. *Successful congregations are arising without purchasing property.*[22] Instead, money is invested in competent staff. A team of three to five people with skills in preaching, music, small groups, and nurturing are given responsibility for bringing new life to a certain area rather than establishing a church. They move to a larger place when they outgrow their facilities. These communities have tremendous flexibility because they do not have a fixed mortgage payment. During its first eight years, New Hope Community Church in Portland, Oregon, worshiped in twelve different locations.

The two-year-old Kensington Community Church in Kensington, Michigan, worships with eight hundred people in a rented building on Sunday and holds weekday teaching sessions in another rented building five miles away. A church in Indiana owns the facilities in which it worships, but conducts a day-care ministry in a leased facility three blocks away. A Nazarene congregation rents retail space for one fifth the cost of a traditional church structure. A medium-size Baptist congregation is purchasing a sporting goods store at one half its value. A huge nondenominational congregation bought a thirty million dollar shopping center for eight million dollars.

These secular structures have a remarkable appeal to the younger, unchurched generation. The people are not intimidated by symbols they do not understand. They sit in theater chairs similar to the movies. Parking is adequate. The facilities can be expanded on site as the congregation grows without having to go through long, extended building programs. Most of all, these facilities are visible, accessible, and convenient.

Paradigm communities that own property often take advantage of any opportunity to conduct worship services in secular places. During the opening of the largest mall in America, the Woodale Baptist Church in Burnsville, Minnesota, negotiated to hold their Sunday worship in the 4.2 million square foot mall.

3. *Congregations often avoid any geographical reference in their*

names. Van Nuys Baptist Church changed its name to Shepherd of the Hills in an attempt to draw from more than one community. Some of the most common replacements for *church* are *community, center, cathedral, chapel, temple, house, and fellowship.* [23]

4. *The word* **church** *is often dropped from the congregation's public name. Church* carries too much unhealthy baggage to be relevant in the emerging new world. Its usage conjures up too many impressions that are major obstacles to the unchurched. Long-time church members subconsciously think of the word *church* as the building (a practice encouraged by the use of the church building on the bulletin cover or stationery). For too many people, building a church means constructing a facility rather than building a community of people who have a mission of bringing new life to an area.

An example of the negative connotation of *church* occurred in Oregon when a congregation dropped the word *church* from its name and inserted the word *fellowship.* Over the next few years the congregation grew rapidly. A new pastor arrived and changed the name back to include the word *church* and the congregation began to decline. Simply changing the name is not all that caused the decline. The overall style of ministry offered by those who dropped or added *church* to the name certainly had as much impact as the baggage that goes with the word. But the word *church* did turn people away.

5. *Denominational identity is avoided in advertising.* The success of businesses like fast-food restaurants is the consistency of their products. A person knows what to expect at each fast-food restaurant around the world. Like a dissatisfied customer, an unchurched person who has a bad experience while visiting a church of a particular denomination is not very likely to try another congregation of the same denomination.

CHAPTER 7

What Ever Happened to the Sunday Church?

I am about to do a new thing . . . do you not perceive it?

ISA. 43:19a

Effective ministry today takes place every day of the week in para-digm communities. During most of the life of North American Christianity, congregational activity was confined to Sunday morning and evening and perhaps Wednesday night. Facilities were designed to be used one or two days a week. Most of the parking was available only on Sunday. The thriving congregations must have adequate weekday space and parking.

PARADIGM ONE

Weekday Ministries Overshadow the Importance of Sunday

Today, two to three times more people participate in paradigm communities during the week than on Sunday. More and more, the social needs of Christians are being fulfilled within the Christian community. From counseling to child care, participants look to their spiritual community for help all week long.

1. *Single adults will be the largest weekday mission field in the twenty-first century.*[1] By the middle of this decade, one half of the population will be single. Large paradigm communities are filled with singles.[2] But these single adults are more different than ever before. Many have never been married and may

97

not have any intention of ever marrying. Some are divorced with no children. Some have children and may or may not be divorced. Some are broken. Some are frantic to find a mate. Some are delirious about being single. Some do not consider themselves single; others define their life as single.

The apostle Paul can help us better understand the importance of the single Christian. According to Paul, being married is not the goal for every person, nor is the family the primary way to define life in the Christian faith. Over the centuries, Christianity has been caricatured as a family-oriented faith, which is far from the truth. Many congregations do not perceive single adults as acceptable spiritual leaders. They are not perceived as mature as married people. Many congregations act as if a spouse is part of the clergy package. We simply have placed too much emphasis on family and marriage. Christianity has no more to do with being married and having a family than it does with being single.

Congregations solely for singles are beginning to emerge. Christ Church in Ft. Lauderdale, Florida, began a worship service just for singles on Easter 1990. Almost two hundred singles attended the first service, even though minimal advertising was done. By May, almost three hundred singles were attending. Later the same year, the congregation received the first full-time pastor to Florida's first singles' congregation. As of 1992, the congregation and staff are still a vital congregation. A similar congregation is found at the First United Methodist Church in Memphis.

Some singles need to have strong leadership positions within the congregation. Others want a safe place to find a mate. Others need a safe place where they can be themselves. Most singles ministries include social events and opportunities for learning three or four times a week. Friday and Saturday night worship services followed by dinner and fellowship are growing in popularity with singles.

2. *Christian child care from the cradle to high school is the second-largest weekday ministry until the second decade of the twenty-first*

century. Lyle Schaller says that most of the growing congregations in the twenty-first century will have schools.[3] Several factors make child-care ministries important. Public school systems will continue to decline in excellence. Gang violence will continue to distract teachers from their primary task. Private enterprise will develop their schools to train people for the jobs they need, paving the way for more private schools at all levels geared toward specific purposes. As religious values continue to be removed from public schools, working parents who have little time to spend with their children will look for private religious schools to instill those values in their children. A school voucher system will increase this trend.

Already, more than fourteen thousand child-care systems are housed in congregations across America. The Southern Baptist Convention is the largest investor in child care with four thousand centers. Regrettably, only 56 percent of these centers are run by the local church, and only 13 percent of these churches (with the exception of the Southern Baptists) list *spiritual development* as one of the three primary goals of their program.[4] It is poor stewardship to allow outside groups to run a weekday child development program in congregational facilities. The Christian community is not a professional babysitter. Congregations should provide child-care ministries to introduce children to Jesus Christ and to develop relationships with the parents instead of renting facilities to an outside organization. As the parents experience the basic transitions of life (many of which cause them to turn to a congregation for help), they naturally think of the congregation that took care of their child.[5]

The director of these weekday schools understands that the weekday ministry is an extension of Christian education. This person is a member of the regular staff and works for the congregation instead of a separate board or committee. Room equipment and supplies are shared by school and congregation. In affluent areas all net income goes into the congregation's budget to support other ministries that cannot support themselves, and scholarships are provided for those who cannot afford the school. In other areas weekday child-care ministries are subsidized by the congregation as part of its mission budget.

Some people oppose private Christian schools on the basis that they undermine the integrity of public schools and leave them to deteriorate even further. Perhaps. But our schools are barely functioning. Red tape piles up on teachers. Christian values are removed from the classroom. Guards are needed in most schools for safety. Children spend much of their time in day-care warehouses without any spiritual development. Something must change. Over the next fifty years public school education could be replaced by private education funded jointly by the government and business.

CAUTION: The crack in history will be known as the "Age of Litigation." Congregations must take great care to avoid costly lawsuits involving child sexual abuse and simple neglect. Some simple rules to follow are: Do not allow volunteers to work in a church-sponsored nursery, child-care center, vacation Bible school, or other youth programs unless they have been attending for at least six months; always have at least two adult workers present in a child-care setting; volunteers and paid workers must be properly screened, especially to determine whether the applicant has ever been arrested or convicted of criminal child abuse (Alaska requires that employers discreetly ask applicants whether they have been sexually abused themselves); and always require references.[6]

3. *Weekday Bible studies and retreats are reducing the prominence of Sunday school.* Bible study is more important today than denominational doctrine. Memorization of Scripture is essential. People need blueprints by which to live the Christian life. Helping people apply the Scripture to their daily needs and relationships is more important than subscribing to the distinctive beliefs of a denomination.

Between 1970 and 1990, Sunday school participation in

mainline denominations declined by 55 percent. Sunday school is becoming increasingly archaic in a time when family patterns are changing. Sunday school makes less sense today: Our world demands a seven-day-a-week community of faith; the name *Sunday school* carries much baggage; so much is forced into forty-five minutes before or after worship; people no longer are willing to devote three hours on Sunday morning.

More and more paradigm communities are replacing the name *Sunday school* with names like *Promised Land* or *Treasure Island* and are working primarily with children on Sunday. (Do not confuse these communities with churches that have Sunday school for children only and ignore adult education.[7]) Often Christian education for adults is on a week night or in the small home groups. Paradigm communities are discovering that people will give large blocks of time on a night during the week more easily than on Sunday. This time is also more productive since it spans more than one hour.

In time Sunday school may disappear. For now, however, congregations need to discover ways to strengthen adult participation in Sunday school while exploring alternate methods of adult Christian education.

Retreats are becoming important avenues for spiritual formation. One weekend experience can accomplish more spiritual transformation than fifty-two short-term Sunday school classes. It is no coincidence that movements like Emmaus are a growing phenomenon across the country.

4. *Innovation will keep weekday ministries in constant flux.* Urban ministries will flourish in the early twenty-first century. More inner-city congregations will follow the lead of the True Vine Missionary Baptist Church and organize to drive out the pushers and teach twelve-step programs that release people from addictions.[8] A Pentecostal church in Brooklyn began a street and bus ministry to children in one of the nation's worst ghettos. They bus eight thousand children to one of North America's largest Sunday schools.

Social justice ministries will grow in prominence as the planet continues to deteriorate. One of the largest Episcopal churches west of the Mississippi has a strong social justice ministry that involves an Interfaith Center to Reverse the Arms Race, two hospitality centers that offer food, shelter, counseling. Their Office of Creative Connections provides a network for attacking urban problems and for managing a thirty-unit inner-city residence and the largest AIDS center based in a congregation. The experience of All Saints Episcopal Church suggests that liberal mainline churches that do well in the twenty-first century will be socially oriented rather than oriented to teaching and nurture.

By the second decade of the twenty-first century, junior high, middle aged, and seniors' ministries will replace children's ministries in their importance to the growth of the congregation. The first wave of baby boomers begins to turn forty years old in 1986; the last wave of boomers turns forty in 2004. In 2014 the last boomer turns fifty. Turning fifty will be devastating and life-altering for boomers. They will be stunned when their body parts start working less efficiently and their skin does not quickly return to its original position. Unlike their predecessors, boomers will expect retirement to provide them with meaning and purpose. Seminars in mid-life crises and grandparent ministries will flourish. By the early 2000s, Christian day-care centers for the elderly will be as important as Christian child care is today. Congregations building children's facilities today need to construct them so that they can be used for elder care tomorrow. Congregations will develop retirement villages that offer opportunities for both fun and a purpose for living. Women's ministries will replace the denominational women's groups.[9] They will focus on helping women balance a career and home, potty train the children, and blend three families into one (hers, his, and theirs). The positions filled by these women will be more than teaching Sunday school or working as youth sponsors.

Intentional, organized prayer ministries are flourishing in

growing communities. They do not assume that people will pray; they show them how and give them opportunities to exercise their gift of prayer. Learning how to pray is one of the major components of the small groups. Prayer vigils are common. Groups meet to pray before, during, and after worship. Intercessory prayer ministries are conducted seven days a week. Prayer hot lines are staffed by trained volunteers. Dr. Ed Young, pastor of Second Baptist Church in Houston, Texas, gives credit for their tremendous growth to their prayer ministries (from one thousand to twelve thousand in worship from 1979 to 1989). Someone is praying at the congregation twenty-four hours a day. Security guards ensure the safety of those praying all night in the prayer room. Each year Second Baptist sponsors two congregations "Schools of Prayer," and annual prayer banquet to honor all the workers in the prayer ministry. Twice each month a one-hour prayer orientation is held to teach new members who work and pray in the twenty-four hour prayer room. Second Baptist's prayer hot line is open twenty-four hours a day as well.

Healing services will continue to grow in popularity. The Vineyard Christian Fellowship Church, begun by John Wimber in 1977, is built on an intense belief in healing. By 1991, the number of Vineyard churches totaled five hundred with a membership of over one hundred thousand. Mainline denominations have experimented with healing services but have not had many positive results because they emphasize the spiritual side of healing and avoid the physical side. Paradigm communities emphasize both sides of healing.

Engagement counseling is becoming a major ministry. Instead of just marrying anyone who comes along, or declining to marry nonmembers, or charging nonmembers an arm and a leg, couples are required to spend a certain amount of time in pastoral counseling and classes in Christian instruction. Tests are administered to help them consider their personal differences and similarities. Marriage enrichment seminars are growing in popularity.

Experiments in forms of worship will continue. The Community of Joy in Asheville, North Carolina, began in 1990 in the basement of a mainstream church. Worship was built around art displays that were explained by a different local artist each week. In two years the services outgrew the space, and when the mother church was not willing to provide more space, the group left to form the Community of Joy.

Week-night worship services will continue to grow as the growing service industries require more people to work on the weekend. Already one third of North Americans work on the weekends. More congregations will follow the example of Willow Creek Community Church and establish week-night services for those already committed to Christ and interested in growing deeper in their faith.

Black congregations will become the largest congregations in North America. The fastest growing denomination in the United States today is the Church of God in Christ, a black Pentecostal denomination with almost four million members.[10] The largest worship auditorium in this nation (with a capacity of 10,400) is owned by the Crenshaw Christian Center in Los Angeles, a primarily black congregation with a black pastor.

Addiction ministries such as alcohol, AIDS, and substance abuse will become the most productive opportunities for congregations to build relationships with the unchurched. Twelve-step programs of all descriptions are springing up everywhere. Transitional ministries are developed for those going through divorce, the loss of a spouse or job, and so forth. One of the largest mainline churches in North America discovered the importance of addiction ministries in the early 1950s. The pastor spent much of his time working with alcoholics. Today the worship attendance remains over five thousand because the pastor had both the physical and spiritual needs of the people in mind.[11]

Hands-on missions at home will become as important as sending money to world missions. People are becoming more interested in being participants in missions instead of specta-tors who send money. Short-term lay missionaries both at home and abroad are replacing many of the traditional life-long missionaries. With fewer and fewer people finding per-sonal fulfillment from their jobs, the need is increasing for opportunities that result in personal fulfillment.

Many communities are offering a variety of short-term mis-sion experiences.[12] These projects are supported best when they arise out of individual participants' concerns, are close enough for personal involvement, show tangible results, and can be held accountable financially. Large amounts for mis-sions can be raised by giving frequent permission to small clusters within the community of faith to raise as much money for their projects as they are able.

Three factors are changing the way paradigm communities are raising money for missions. First, people no longer give all their money to one cause. More and more people give to causes outside their church. Second, people see little reason today to send money away to foreign missions when so many local needs go unmet. Third, many adults prefer to give money to projects in which they can be physically involved.

As discretionary assets and the World Wars I and II genera-tions die, money given to nonprofit organizations will dwin-dle. Many congregations will find that endowments for mis-sions and ministry will be essential to the twenty-first century. Endowments must be tools to thrive on rather than to survive on. Endowments set aside for maintenance and facilities are not proving to be healthy, nor will they inspire giving in the twenty-first century.

CHAPTER 8

Three Essential Ingredients of Paradigm Communities

*Do not be conformed to this world, but be transformed
by the renewing of your minds.*

ROM. 12:2

*Paradigm communities place a high priority on biblical integrity,
evangelism, and quality.* They avoid superficial biblical criticism. Quality is a passion that is felt and taught at every level
of ministry. And everything is done in the name of evangelism. These three ingredients are present in all paradigm
communities.

Biblical Integrity Is Everything

Paradigm communities receive their marching orders from
the Scriptures. They focus on the Scriptures rather than gim-
micks or programs that cause growth in attendance. Everything they do is based on their interpretation of Scriptures.
And they are more conservative in their interpretation of
Scriptures than most Protestants have been the last thirty
years.[1]

But their conservatism has a new but old twist. Grace is
emphasized. Paradigm communities are avoiding making the
mistakes of spiritual imperialism and the bigotry of many
evangelical expressions of faith in the past. Guilt is replaced
with an emphasis on compassion and forgiveness. Judgment
is left to God. Compassion is more important than doctrine.

Each person is seen as an individual who is the object of God's love and therefore the object of each Christian's love. These communities focus on the good within each person without compromising the good news. They realize that unity of purpose is more important than uniformity of belief. Unity of the Body of Christ is the goal. This is accomplished without everyone looking, acting, and thinking alike.

Evangelism Is Everything

Paradigm communities have one agenda—to evangelize the entire world to faith in Jesus Christ. Those who worship are welcomed as they are, but those who join and those who give leadership must acknowledge Jesus Christ as Lord and Master and be willing to serve as a servant rather than a church official.

1. *Evangelizing an area is the goal instead of building a local church.* Paradigm communities view everyone in the total population of their area as part of their responsibility rather than just those who attend or comprise the membership. With this kind of orientation, no one ever asks, How large should our church become? Or, What is the best size for a church? They know that a community of faith never reaches the point of not being able to reach out any further. The leadership knows that the moment a congregation ceases to expend itself on behalf of the spiritual and physical redemption to those around them, it ceases to be the Body of Christ and becomes like the ingrown religious crowd in the Old and New Testaments.

They target the people in their area they primarily want to reach. They use sophisticated demographic studies to point out the bulk and life-style of the unchurched people within their area. Saddleback Valley Community Church has gone so far as to actually draw up a picture of the type of person they have targeted. They call him *Saddleback Sam.* Willow Creek Community Church talks about *Unchurched Harry* and *Unchurched Mary.*

Often, these communities target people in the area that have given up on organized religion. Either they have been turned off by a bad experience or have been burned out. These congregations make no attempt to hide the fact that they welcome people disgruntled or disinterested in the religion. The facilities do not look like a church, nothing in the worship is traditional, and the printed material clearly welcomes those who have given up on religion.[2]

2. *Paradigm communities are radical in their commitments to Christ and to one another.* A clear distinction is made between profession of faith in Christ and membership in a local church or denomination. Personal commitment to Christ is emphasized; joining a church or denomination is not emphasized. This commitment to Christ defines the quality of all other relationships. If Christ is put first, then the Body of Christ takes on a new importance. Most of the participants' relationships and social lives revolve around the life of the congregation.

Membership is tied to accepting certain responsibilities. Leaders are asked to put the Body of Christ before their own needs and concerns. Often, tithing and regular service are requirements for joining. The pastors and leaders see what they are doing as essential to both life as we know it and immortality. Faith is worth dying for.

Infant baptism makes less sense in such a setting. Adult baptism is more meaningful than infant baptism. Younger generations expect to experience personally every aspect of their faith. Infant baptism holds no meaning to them as adults, since they did not experience it personally. A greater openness to rebaptism is needed in some traditions as more and more adults wish to experience the emotional power of baptism for themselves.[3] We can no longer assume that children are reared in the church or that their parents will encourage them to discover the meaning of their baptism. Those denominations that encourage infant baptism will have to develop a new interpretation that emphasizes the importance of the future decision of the child in completing the sacrament later in life.

Commitment to Christ comes before family, nation, or wealth. Personal conversion and participation are more important than membership. One community tells its guests each Sunday: If you want to be a participant in our ministry, come forward now and make your intentions known. Some churches never mention joining during worship. Instead, commitment to Jesus Christ is stressed. Individuals interested in joining are discovered in the small home groups where the meaning of membership is spelled out, their spiritual pulse is taken, and an invitation to join is issued. Accountability and service are at the heart of membership. Many communities require people to become involved in ministry before they are invited to join.

Confirmation classes for youth no longer make sense either. We must not continue the mistake of mass entrance into the church begun by Constantine. Children and youth need to be introduced personally to Jesus Christ and experience the cleansing grace of God. New ways must be found to teach our youth and allow them to respond to God's movement in their lives at their own pace.

Long-term training classes for new Christians are crucial. These classes are designed to be as much an experience in spiritual formation as an exposure to doctrine. How a person serves is as important as what a person knows. Servanthood is a measure of leadership. New Christians are introduced to the meaning of servanthood not out of obligation but out of a desire for fulfillment. They are shown how to find their place within the Body of Christ through their service to others.

A successful model for new members is occurring in a mainline congregation in a suburb of St. Louis. People desiring membership are required to take thirteen weeks of training led by both laity and staff. Emphasis is placed on spiritual formation and team building. The group is together long enough that many of the groups go on to become a regular Sunday morning class or small group during the week. Over the past ten years, the congregation has had steady growth in an area where growth is not expected from a mainline church.

Quality Is Paramount

Paradigm communities have a passion for excellence in all that they do. The pastors and laity go out of their way to assure that everything done "in the name of Jesus Christ" is done right, or it is not attempted at all. This passion for excellence is contagious. It inspires others to reach for accomplishments most churches would think impossible. But more important, this attitude brings a feeling of self-worth to everyone involved. In time people do really believe what they read—they "can do all things through Christ who strengthens me" (Phil. 4:13).

Daniel V. Biles of the Alban Institute conducted a study of selected pastors and congregations in the Lutheran Church. He arrived at the following formulas for evaluating excellence as a result of his interviews: (1) Excellence in the congregation is fidelity to the faith in which we are baptized. (2) Excellence is also responsiveness to the environment in which a church ministers. (3) The foundations for excellence are mission, leadership, and lay commitment and ownership. (4) The expressions of excellence are quality worship, quality education, quality care, and outreach.[4]

In short, the critical difference between healthy, growing congregations and other churches is not some secret formula for success. Their distinguishing feature is that they do the common, mundane, boring tasks of ministry uncommonly well. They do so regardless of their size, socioeconomic makeup, location, or environmental changes.[5]

This passion for excellence starts with the role modeling of pastors. It is the basic ingredient to their vision.

One Question for Paradigm Communities

Will paradigm communities mature enough to take seriously the social justice dimension of the biblical witness? In the latter half of the twentieth century, many congregations concentrated on humankind's physical needs almost to the exclusion of their spiritual needs. Tears easily surfaced when faced with physical needs. But seldom were tears shed over the growing spiritual gap between God and the human family. The danger in the twenty-first century is that the pendulum might swing the other direction, and paradigm communities might concern themselves only with getting people ready to meet God and forget that much of the joy of the Christian walk is in this life. Those communities that focus primarily on the spiritual without losing sight of the importance of the physical will do well in the twenty-first century.

We had to face the issue of social justice several times at Colonial Hills. Our involvement in the public arena and our commitment to social justice caused many people either not to join or to fade away over time. Over a ten-year period, several hundred active members joined other congregations because they did not believe their pastor and laity should be involved in the root causes of social justice. Some left over our peace conference with Robert McAfee Brown. Others stormed out because of our work in community organizing. But we continued to be faithful to the gospel.

My largest concern about the future of paradigm communities is that they will never mature to the point of becoming involved in social justice beyond single issue votes such as abortion and homosexuality. Time will tell.

Not an Easy Road to Travel

Dancing with dinosaurs will not be easy. Some will discover that their spiritual toes become too sore to bear, and they will leave before the dance is over. The conflict will be too much to take. Others will not survive the dance. They will be crushed under the weight of the challenges. No serious Christian can ignore that many lives are at stake in the suggestions made in this book.

Developing paradigm communities requires total sacrifice of self and reliance on a power that comes only from God. Such a requirement may cause pastors and laity to reevaluate the seriousness of their commitment.

Some pastors may encounter hardships. Some may lose their jobs. Some pastors may experience great opposition from comfortable laity and bureaucrats. And some may find themselves working longer and harder hours than they expected.

Laity may be forced to reevaluate the level of what they expect from themselves. Implementing these recommendations may mean the end of programs and organizational structures that have served them well for years. They may lead to the closing, merging, and relocating of churches loved by them for years. Some laity may have to decide which is more important—their buildings or their desire to pass on new life in Christ.

Eleven practical suggestions can help leaders develop an effective paradigm community in the twenty-first century. (1) Do not be afraid to dance with the dinosaur. It can be a barrel of fun. Take the risk to allow the Holy Spirit to move you into innovative ministries. (2) Pray and put yourself in a position where God can use you. (3) Listen to what people are saying. Use every conversation outside the four walls of your congregation to evaluate the type of ministries needed to minister today. (4) Develop a vision and recast this vision at every opportunity. (5) Teach people the Scriptures and help them learn how to pray for themselves. (6) Develop a style of ministry that causes laity to be in ministry to one another. Avoid doing ministry for them. Spend most of your time developing trained leaders or equippers of small groups. (7) Study more sociology than theology. Learn how people think and feel and how systems operate. (8) Inspire people to do things that they would never have dreamed possible without your encouragement and support. (9) Target key life-styles within your service area to introduce people to Christ and to nurture them in small groups. (10) Be prepared to risk everything that you have. (11) Above all else, once laity are equipped, get out of the way and let them be the priesthood of God.

NOTES

....

Chapter 1. Bursting Wineskins and Munching Sheep

1. In 1992, the House of Representatives passed a measure that will require all nonprofit organizations to provide photocopies of their annual IRS form 990 informational tax returns to anyone upon request in writing or by telephone (*National & International Religion Report*, Vol. 6, No. 16, July 27, 1992).

Also in 1992, more church versus state cases filled the Supreme Court docket than ever before. Consider the following decisions: Nonsectarian prayers are not permitted because they coerce students into participating in a religious society. A Denver school teacher is constitutionally prohibited from reading the Bible silently during class time while his students read other books, and he is forbidden from including the story of Jesus and the Bible in pictures in a classroom library. Officials in Illinois violated the separation of church and state by endorsing a Catholic mass during an Italian culture festival. Crosses on the city seals of Zion and Rolling Meadows, Illinois, are unconstitutional because they convey government endorsement of religion. A North Carolina judge violated the Constitution by opening his court with prayer. A federal law that allowed workers to avoid union membership for religious reasons is unconstitutional because it forces the government to make a distinction between people based on their religious beliefs (*National & International Religion Report*, Vol. 6, No. 15, July 13, 1992).

2. God created the world and gave it to us to enjoy and care for. God renewed this gift to Abram when God covenanted with Abram to make

him the father of a great nation. God then asked this nation to be a light to other nations. When confined to slavery in Egypt, God sent Moses to remind them of "a land flowing with milk and honey" (Exod. 13:5), where life would be abundant.

In time Israel refused to be a light to the nations, and again God renewed the passion to share this new life in the person of Jesus of Nazareth who told us that he "came that they may have life, and have it abundantly" (John 10:10b). Jesus followed that statement with another—"For those who want to save their life will lose it, and those who lose their life for my sake will find it" (Matt. 16:25). Jesus demonstrated this truth in his death and God confirmed it in his resurrection.

After death and resurrection, Jesus reminded the remaining disciples, "But you will receive power when the Holy Spirit has come upon you; and you will be my witnesses in Jerusalem, in all Judea and Samaria, and to the ends of the earth" (Acts 1:8). Soon after Jesus spoke these words, the New Testament church was born. When it looked as if the early disciples were reluctant to share this gift with the Gentiles, Peter had a dream in which he was called to share the good news with a Greek named Cornelius. And when the remaining disciples chose to remain at Jerusalem rather than go "to the ends of the earth," Saul became Paul and took the message of new life to the ends of his earth.

And so the story goes. God's purpose for creation moves forward in us today.

3. People trained in therapeutic models tend not to do well in a growing congregation. They have trouble holding staff accountable, and when a staff person reaches the point that the congregation outgrows their skills or they refuse to grow further in their learning, the pastor is not able to terminate their employment.

Chapter 2. Caught in a Crack of History

1. For a fascinating look at the future, see Benjamin R. Barber, "Jihad vs. McWorld," *Atlantic Monthly,* March 1992, pp. 53-63.

2. See Alvin Toffler, *Powershift: Knowledge, Wealth, and Violence at the Edge of the 21st Century* (New York: Bantam Books, 1990), p. xix; and Lance Morrow, "Old Paradigm, New Paradigm," *Time,* January 14, 1991, p. 65.

3. See Gerald Celente, *Trend Tracking* (New York: John Wiley & Sons, 1990), pp. 11-18. Pay special attention to Celente's definition of the "Globalnomic" system of tracking trends.

116

4. Even W. Edward Deming, the guru of improvement, says that before improvement takes place most organizations need a paradigm shift in most areas.

5. Many excellent books have been written lately about the tremendous religious and spiritual upheavals occurring in North America. Most important among these works are Kennon Callahan, *Effective Church Leadership* (New York: Harper & Row, 1991); Loren Mead, *The Once and Future Church* (New York: The Alban Institute, 1991); Lyle Schaller, *The Seven-Day-A-Week Church* (Nashville: Abingdon Press, 1992); George Hunter, *How to Reach Secular People* (Nashville: Abingdon Press, 1991). These authors tell us that we live on a mission field instead of a churched society; we are the first generation of North Americans to live in a secular society where most churches go unnoticed and have little influence; we live today in world very similar to that of the first century Christian. Each one of these authors identifies a piece or two of the changing picture of North America. We are indebted to these servants for their courage to state clearly the dilemma of Protestants.

6. See Martin Marty, "Why Is Everybody Always Picking on Evangelicals," *Context,* Vol. 23, No. 6, 1991, pp. 1-3.

7. Shared at a workshop for the Southwest Texas Annual Conference, August 26-28, 1991.

8. In 1991, more than eight hundred Christian leaders representing some fifty denominations petitioned the television networks, stations, and film industries to end the anti-Christian bigotry. See "Christian Leaders Call for End to Anti-Christian Bigotry," *Evangelical Press News Service,* March 15, 1991, p. 1.

9. For more information, read Robert Ellwood, Jr., *Alternative Altars: Unconventional and Eastern Spirituality in America* (Chicago: University of Chicago Press, 1979).

10. For more information, see Martin Marty, "A Special Issue: The Human Genome Project," *Context,* No. 21, 1990, p. 3.

11. Not all futurists or scientists believe this will be the age of discernment. Some believe that the pace of new developments will take quantum leaps in unprecedented new discoveries. But all agree that this is the information age, and whoever controls information controls power.

12. The more science knows the less it's sure it knows. In 1991, the Big Bang theory was discovered to have flaws and astronomers are searching presently for another solution to the mystery of the galaxy. See Michael D. Lemonick, "Bang! A Big Bang Theory May Be Shot," *Time,* January 14, 1991, p. 63.

117

13. Econ-ecofaith is the belief that economics will force the rejuvenation of the planet. When we reach the point that commerce is in danger of becoming impossible, the world's traders will find ways to make environmental measures one of the major forms of commerce. Until that time neither religion nor baby boomers will tackle the environment.

Some feel that technology will be the catalyst for the caring and feeding of the environment (see Martin Marty, *Context,* July 1, 1990, p. 4.). Others feel that religion will be the catalyst (see Russell Chandler, *Racing Toward 2001* [Grand Rapids: Zondervan Publishing House, 1992], p. 78.)

Biocentrics deemphasizes humanity's distinctiveness as the pinnacle of the creation and emphasizes the creative powers of the universe over redemption from sin and the need for personal redemption. The danger of the twenty-first century is that both the New Age movement and the biocentric movement both rival the Christian perspective of God the Creator and replace it with worship of the creation itself. Ecofaith is the movement that proclaims a vision of a "sacred" planet that is to be respected as a creation of God.

Bioethics includes in-vitro fertilization, organ transplants, triage, surrogate parenting, the right to die, fetal tissue, gene surgery, living wills, euthanasia.

14. According to the 1992-93 Barna Report, 24 percent of all men agree that "the whole idea of sin is outdated."

15. John Naisbett, *Megatrends* (New York: Morrow, 1990), pp. 298-309.

16. For more information, see George Barna, *The Frog in the Kettle: What Christians Need to Know about Life in the Year 2000* (Ventura, California: Regal Books, 1990).

17. See Norval D. Glenn, "What Does Family Mean," *American Demographics,* June 1991, pp. 30-36. Also, see Joseph M. Winski, "Who We Are, How We Live, What We Think," *Advertising Age,* January 20, 1992, p. 16.

18. Richard Olsen and Jordan Leonard, Jr., *Ministry with Families in Flux: The Church and Changing Patterns of Life* (Louisville: Westminster/John Knox Press, 1990), p. 85.

19. For more information, see George Gallup, Jr., "Tracking America's Soul," *Christianity Today,* November 17, 1989.

20. For more information, see Theodore J. Gorden, "Technology and the Future of Business," *The Futurist,* May–June 1992, p. 26.

21. See William Schneider, "The Suburban Century Begins," *Atlantic Monthly,* July 1992, pp. 33-44.

22. One percent of the households in America hold one-third of the

country's wealth. One out of three white households reported an income of over $100,000 in 1988. See Robert Pear, "Rich Got Richer in the 80's; Others Held Even," *New York Times,* January 10, 1991, pt. A, p. 1. See also Tom Sine, *Wild Hope* (Dallas: Word Publishing, 1991), p. 41.

23. For more information, see Neil Howe and William Strauss, "The New Generation Gap," *Atlantic Monthly,* December 1992, pp. 67- 89.

24. See Naula Black, *Shifting Gears: Thriving in the New Economy* (Collins Canada, Harper, 1990).

25. John Naisbett, *Megatrends 2000* (New York: Morrow, 1990), pp. 118- 153.

26. For more information, see the 1992 editions of *American Demographics.*

27. For more information, read John K. Urice, "The Next Century: The Impact of Social and Economic Trends on the Arts in Education," *Design for Arts in Education,* May–June 1989, p. 37.

28. James H. Shonk, *Team Based Organizations* (Homewood, Ill.: Business One Irwin, 1992). Rich Maurer, *Caught in the Middle* (Cambridge: Productivity Press, 1992).

29. For more information, see Alvin Toffler, *Powershift,* p. 226.

30. For more information, see Michael Kami, *Trigger Points* (New York: McGraw Hill, 1988), pp. 21-36. Also see John Naisbett, *Megatrends* (New York: Morrow, 1990), chaps. 3, 4, and 6.

31. Russell Chandler, *Racing Toward 2001: The Forces Shaping America's Religious Future* (Grand Rapids: Zondervan Publishing House, 1992), p. 124.

32. See Arthur D. Little, "What Executives Need to Learn," *Prism,* Fourth Quarter, 1990.

33. See Gerald Celente, *Trend Tracking* (New York: John Wiley & Sons, 1990) and Neil Postman, *Amusing Ourselves to Death; Public Discourse in the Age of Show Business* (New York: Penguin Books, 1986).

34. For more information, see Judy Daubenmier, Associated Press, "Education: Up to a Million American Families Maintain Home-School Where Their Children Are Taught," *Los Angeles Times* (Bulldog Edition), March 11, 1990, pt. A, p. 27.

35. Waldrop, "You'll Know It's the 21st Century," *American Demographics,* pp. 23-27.

36. See John Naisbett, *Megatrends 2000* (New York: Morrow, 1990), pp. 216- 239.

37. Two books providing a good look into the emerging world through the eyes of women are the following: Nell Morton, *The Jour-*

ney Home (Boston: Beacon Press, 1985) and Rosemary Radford Ruether, *Sexism and God-Talk: Toward a Feminist Theology* (Boston: Beacon Press, 1983).

38. For a description of "Clue management," see Michael J. Kami, *Trigger Points* (New York: McGraw Hill, 1988), pp. 89, 148-151. Clue management is looking between the lines to detect trends. It is "thinking laterally to transform and adapt seemingly unrelated facts." Kami also suggests that we not make forecasts about the future, but instead make assumptions.

39. William McKinney, "From the Center to the Margins," *Books & Religion*, Winter 1989, p. 3.

Chapter 3. The Fringe People

1. Walter Kiechel, "The Leader as Servant," *Fortune Magazine*, May 4, 1992, p. 121.

2. See Michael Kami, *Trigger Points* (New York: McGraw Hill, 1988), pp. 37-42.

3. Peter Drucker, *Managing for the Future* (New York: Penguin Books, 1992).

4. For more information about excellence, innovation, and anticipation, see Joel Barker, *Future Edge* (New York: Morrow, 1992).

5. Tradition does not need long to choke out the new life God so freely offers to those who offer it to others. The Pharisees came into existence less than sixty years before Jesus was born, yet their power and authority suggests that they had existed for centuries.

6. Many Christian leaders do not want to consider triage because one of the assumptions in the paradigm is that *nice* equals *Christian*. Many are so codependent they are unable to make life and death decisions. As a result, many people who could be helped are lost in the crack.

7. Lyle Schaller, "The Big Boxes Are Coming," *Net Results*, August, 1992, pp. 6-7.

8. Los Angeles, Dallas-Ft. Worth, Houston, Atlanta, Florida-West Central, Phoenix, Seattle, San Francisco, Memphis, and Denver are the metropolitan areas that contain the majority of the congregations growing by more than one hundred in worship per year. Source: John N. Vaughn, "North America's Fastest Growing Churches 1989–90," *Church Growth Today*, Vol. 7, No. 1, prt. 2, 1992.

9. According to Lyle Schaller, four hundred fifty is a critical mass for moving forward into one of the largest churches of the twenty-first cen-

tury. His book, *The Seven-Day-A-Week Church* (Nashville: Abingdon Press, 1991), describes the many reasons for this number. This book is perhaps Schaller's best book to date.

Chapter 4. Leading the Sheep Back to Pasture

1. Alvin Toffler, *Powershift* (New York: Bantam, 1990), p. 3.

2. "The Wall Street Journal," November 20, 1991, pp. A1, A6.

3. After the first century, the basic ministry of the church was increasingly turned inward for the sake of the communities rather than remaining as a tool to evangelize the world. For more information, see J.N.D. Kelly, *Early Christian Doctrines* (San Francisco: Harper, 1978), p. 219. Also see J. G. Davies, "The Disintegration of the Christian Initiation Rite," *Theology*, 1947.

4. The apostolic fathers included Clement of Rome, Ignatius, Polycarp, the author of 2 Clement, Barnabus, Hermas, Justin, Aristides, Tatian Athenagoras, and Theophilus.

5. This is the first way of describing the early Christians. They followed the Way, Jesus Christ.

6. The stoning of Stephen in Acts 7:59 is one example. On numerous occasions Paul was imprisoned.

7. M. Scott Peck, *The Different Drum* (New York: Simon and Schuster, 1987), p. 59.

8. E. Mansel Pattison, *Pastor and Parish—A Systems Approach* (Philadelphia: Fortress Press, 1977), p. 19.

9. References to *the home* are located throughout the New Testament including Mark 2:1; 7:14-27; 9:33; Matt.13:26; Mark 14:14; and Luke 10.

10. Paul refers twice to the Church of God in Corinth: I Cor. 1:2 and II Cor. 1:1.

11. In Acts 20:6-12 Paul's visit to Troas caused the house groups to gather to break bread and to hear Paul teach them.

12. The Greek word for "church" is *ekklesia* which means "called out."

13. In Acts 1:8, Jesus said, "You will be my witnesses in Jerusalem, in all Judea and Samaria, and to the ends of the earth." Peter's sermon in the book of Acts sets forth the basic message of the early church. Also see Acts 1:14-36.

14. God had the same plan for Israel, but she refused. Israel was chosen and called out of Egypt to be a "light to the nations." God's problem with Israel was that she felt she was chosen because she was special. God reminded her over and over that she was special only

because she was chosen for a mission. Israel was constantly reminded that she had a responsibility to care for the "stranger at the gate." But Israel came to believe that she was chosen because she was special.

15. In Acts 16:16-24, Paul took time to heal the demented woman on his way to the temple to pray. He had passed by her on several occasions, but this time he stopped. In Acts 10:1-31, Peter dealt with the subject of prejudice within the context of bringing new life to the Gentile Cornelius. In Philemon Paul overlooks the fact that the recipient owns a slave. These examples in no way excuse us from being concerned with social justice is ultimately meaningless if individuals are not experiencing new life in Christ.

16. This simple statement was not all there was to the faith of these early communities. Catechumen exercises soon became considered to be essential, but they were never considered automatically to be the beginning point of faith.

17. Stuart G. Hall, *Doctrine and Practice in the Early Church* (Grand Rapids, Mich.: Eerdmans, 1991), p. 21. Hall makes mention of the Marcionites as the non-orthodox.

18. Acts 2:38; 3:6, 16; 4:10, 18; 5:31-32, 42; 7:54-56, 59; 10:46-48; 13:27-33; 15:26; 16:18, 31; 18:5, 28; 19:4-5, 13, 17; 20:21; 21:13; 22:8; 28:31.

19. Oscar Cullmann, *The Earliest Christian Confessions*, trans. by J. K. S. Reild (London: Lutterworth Press, 1949), chaps. 2, 3, and 4.

20. *Creeds of the Churches*, edited by John H. Leith (Louisville: John Knox Press, 1982 ed.), p. 3.

21. C. H. Dodd, *The Apostolic Preaching and Its Developments*, p. 17.

22. Corwin, Virginia, *St. Ignatius and Christianity in Antioch* (New Haven: Yale University Press, 1960).

23. J. D. Kelly, *Early Christian Doctrines*, revised edition (Harper Collins, New York, 1978), p. 29. For a detailed discussion of the development of Christology, see pages 137-62.

24. Interrogatory Creed of Hippolytus (A.D. 215), Creed of Marcellus (A.D. 240), Creed of Caesarea (A.D. 325) and The Nicean Creed (A.D. 325). The Apostles' Creed was finalized sometime between A.D. 710 and A.D. 724. All of these texts are far too removed from the early church to be of any value to us in our setting.

25. See Romans 6:3, Galatians 3:27, and I Cor. 12:13.

26. Four basic texts give the context out of which the practice of spiritual gifts emerges—Rom. 12:1-8, I Cor. 12:1-27, I Cor. 14:1-5, Eph. 4:1-7, 11-16, and I Pet. 4:8-11.

27. Read Acts 5 for a graphic story of the extent of New Testament accountability.

28. For a complete account of this event see Acts 14–16. See also the account of Peter's vision in Acts 10.

29. Adapted from *Cell Church Magazine*, Vol. 1, Number 2, p. 2.

Chapter 5. The Demise of the Program-based Church

1. Of course, small group ministries have been around a long time. In the seventeenth century, John Wesley vigorously promoted class meetings. Under the direction of Lyman Coleman, Serendipity has promoted small groups for several decades. In 1992, Ralph Neighbor's Touch Outreach Ministries celebrated its tenth year of equipping congregations for small group ministries.

2. William M. Easum, *The Church Growth Handbook* (Nashville: Abingdon Press, 1990).

3. Small group ministries are nothing new; John Wesley promoted class meetings. But over time, with the emergence of a more educated and less itinerate clergy, the class meetings died off. There is new movement among United Methodists toward renewing the class meetings under the title of Covenant Discipleship.

4. Elmer Towns, *10 of Today's Most Innovative Churches* (Ventura, California: Regal, 1990), p. 235.

5. For more information, read Dale Galloway, *20/20 Vision* (Portland: Scott Publishing, 1986).

6. Interview with Dale Galloway, November 8, 1992, Seattle, Washington.

7. Materials for the Telecare Ministry can be purchased by writing New Hope Community Church, Portland, Oregon.

8. Carl George, *Prepare Your Church for the Future* (New York: Fleming H. Revell Company, 1991).

9. Carl George, interview at the Leadership Network gathering, August, 1991, Denver.

10. A six-part video series describing the process at Ginghamsburg can be purchased from Media Resources for Ministry, United Theological Seminary, 1810 Harvard Blvd., Dayton, Ohio 45406. Or call 1-800-322-5817.

11. Dr. Mike Slaughter, from the front cover of an advertisement featuring Dr. Slaughter's environment for renewal.

12. Ralph Neighbor, *Where Do We Go From Here?* (Houston: Touch Publications, 1990), p. 405. Pastors wishing to make this transition should read chapter 26.

13. Congregations interested in more information can contact Ralph Neighbor at Touch Outreach Ministries, Box 19888, Houston, Tex. 77224.

14. Program-based congregations wishing to transition to cell-based model may contact North Star Strategies, 1500 N. Lincoln, Urbana, Ill. 61801 in care of Jim Egli or call 217-384-3070.

15. *Cell Church Magazine,* Box 19888, Houston, Tex. 77224. Also "Cell Church," 14925 Memorial Drive, Suite 101, Houston, Tex. 77079.

16. Neighbor, *Where Do We Go From Here?*

17. Jürgen Moltmann, *Hope for the Church* (Nashville: Abingdon Press, 1979), pp. 21, 34.

18. More than 30 percent of the pastors of congregations with over two thousand members are not seminary trained. See *Newscope,* March 6, 1992, p. 2.

19. Willow Creek Community Church has developed the most comprehensive gifts inventory system I have seen. You can obtain a copy of it from Fuller Institute by ordering "Networking," Fuller Institute, Box 919901, Pasadena, Cal. 91109, or by calling 1-800-999-9578. The cost is $67.95. Fuller also has several other models. A shorter and less labor intense model is provided by Net Press, "Identifying Your Spiritual Giftabilities." Write 5001 Avenue N., Lubbock, Tex. 79412.

20. The basic texts for spiritual gifts are Eph. 4, Rom. 12, I Cor. 12, and I Pet. 4.

21. Davida Foy Crabtree, *The Empowering Church* (New York: Alban Institute, 1989), p. 6. However, the entire book offers many suggestions about workplace ministries.

22. For more information on the new structure, see *How to Reach Baby Boomers,* by William M. Easum (Nashville: Abingdon Press, 1991), pp. 58-63.

23. William H. Willimon and Robert L. Wilson, *Rekindling the Flame* (Nashville: Abingdon Press, 1987), p. 47.

24. See Galloway, *20/20 Vision.*

25. See Neighbor, *Where Do We Go from Here?* p. 75.

26. *Fortune Magazine,* April 22, 1991, p. 80.

27. Several Annual Conferences of The United Methodist Church have done studies on the effectiveness of nonordained pastors in small congregations. North Indiana Conference is one. Their studies show a remarkable difference.

At the Southwest Texas Annual Conference several examples were cited from 1991–1992 of nonordained pastors outperforming clergy in small congregations. The problem is that once these people show they have the skills to lead the congregation forward, denominational leaders want to send them to school to become accredited. The things they will learn in these schools are the very things that are killing the denomination. It would be far better to allow them to work on the staff of a large congregation where they can learn functional rather than doctrinal skills.

28. Shared at a workshop for the Southwest Texas Annual Conference of The United Methodist Church, August 1992.

Chapter 6. A Reformation in Worship

1. Cited in *Ten of Today's Most Innovative Churches,* by Elmer Towns (Ventura, Calif.: Regal, 1990), p. 60.

2. For an example of contemporary worship, order "Demonstrations of Contemporary Worship," a video of music from the Colonial Hills United Methodist Church. They will also include a written copy of the service and two additional forms of worship. Cost is $39.95. Write the Perkins School of Theology, Southern Methodist University, Dallas, Tex., 75275 or call 1-214-692-2251.

3. The following material offers excellent guides for developing twenty-first century worship: Worship Leader, Box 40985, Nashville, Tenn. 37204; House of Worship (a newsletter), 1-800-245-7664, $29.95 a year; Banners, 1-615-791-0800; Bring a Friend Sunday, Net Press, 5001 Avenue N., Lubbock, Tex. 79412; 1-800-638-3463; Growth Plus Worship Attendance Crusade Guide, Discipleship Resources, Box 189, Nashville, Tenn. 37202, 1-615-340-7285.

4. One of the primary reasons Eastern religions and the New Age movement interests so many disinfranchised Christians is due to the loss of mystery in our worship. Everything is too rational. Faith was never meant to be rational.

5. This clean-up generation is referred to most often as baby busters but they are far from being a bust generation. Numerically, this generation outnumbers baby boomers, but they will outvote the boomers in the late 1990s. For more information, see Neil Howe & William Strauss, "The New Generation Gap," *Atlantic Monthly,* December 1992, pp. 67-89.

6. Herb Miller, "Sing the Wondrous Story," *Net Results,* November, 1991, p. 3.

7. Doug Murren, *The Baby Boomerang: Catching Baby Boomers as They Return to Church* (Ventura, Calif: Regal, 1990), p. 189.

8. John Bisagno, *How to Build an Evangelistic Church* (Nashville: Broadman Press, 1971), p. 71.

9. Write Christian Copyright Licensing, Inc. 6130 N.E. 78th Ct. Suite C-11, Portland, Ore. 97218 or call 1-800-234-2446. Congregations wishing to make their own slides should make them in reverse negative so

that the background is black and the words white. Otherwise the words are difficult to see in the daylight.

10. For examples of indigenous music used during worship, contact Hosanna Music, 1-800-877-4443; Maranatha Music, 1-800-444-4012 or 1-800-245-76643; Saddleback Praises, 1-800-458-BSSB; Brentwood Music (for slides), 1-800-333-9000; Bethel Chapel, Box 51, Brentwood, Tenn. 37024.

11. James Emery White, "Singing a New Song," *Growing Churches* (Sunday School Board of the Southern Baptist Convention, 127 Ninth Avenue, Nashville, Tenn.)? Oct., Nov., Dec. quarter, 1992, p. 44.

12. C. Kirk Hadaway, *Church Growth Principles: Separating Fact from Fiction* (Nashville: Broadman Press, 1991), p. 67.

13. Gustave Niebuhr, "So It Isn't Rock of Ages, It Is Rock, And Many Love It," *The Wall Street Journal,* December 1991, p. A.

14. *National & International Religion Report,* June 1, 1992, Vol. 6, No. 12.

15. These dramas can be ordered from Fuller Institute, P.O. Box 919901, Pasadena, Calif. 91109; 1-800-999-9578.

16. For more information, see Bert Decker, *You've Got to Be Believed to Be Heard* (New York: St. Martin's Press, 1992).

17. Satellite ministries are not new to mainline Protestants. The earliest forms of vacation Bible schools were expressions of satellite ministries. Instead of waiting for people to come to the church, vacation Bible school went to them. Over time, these Bible schools were institutionalized, held on the church property, and designed mostly for members.

18. Harry D. Williams, "Churches Must Offer Newer Options," *California Southern Baptist,* May 17, 1990, p. 6. For a thorough examination of the secular, biblical, sociological, cultural, and logistical aspects of multiple-site ministries, see Elmer Town, *Ten of Today's Most Innovative Churches* (Ventura, Calif.: Regal Books, 1991).

19. These ministries do not relocate because relocation seldom results in developing a large, strong congregation for the twenty-first century. Too many generational obstacles are carried to the new site.

20. Cited from an interview with Gerald Martin, Cornerstone Church, 265 W. Springbook Road Broadway, Harrisonburg, Virginia. The congregation is based on the cell model. The guide Cornerstone uses to develop this lay ministry is the *Shepherd's Guide Book,* by Ralph Neighbor. The book can be purchased through Touch Outreach Ministries, Box 19888, Houston, Tex. 77224.

21. Perimeter Church is a member of The Presbyterian Church in America. This denomination was organized in 1973 with 249 congregations and 40,000 members. Today it has 1,200 congregations and over

217,000 members. The denomination is conservative and highly committed to the Church Growth movement. Their goal is to have 875 new congregations by the end of the century.

22. See Lyle Schaller, *44 Questions for Church Planters* (Nashville: Abingdon Press, 1991).

23. Lyle Schaller, *The Seven-Day-A-Week Church* (Nashville: Abingdon Press, 1992), p. 35.

Chapter 7. What Ever Happened to the Sunday Church?

1. See Jerry Jones, ed., *Single Adult Ministries* (Colorado Springs: Navpress, 1991); Harry Odum, *The Vital Singles Ministry* (Nashville: Abingdon Press, 1992).

2. The largest singles ministry in North America occurs in Second Baptist Church in Houston, Texas. Over fourteen hundred singles gather each week in the twenty-two classes offered for singles on Sunday. Over eight hundred fifty singles attend classes each week at the First Baptist Church in Jacksonville, Florida. The church even developed a twelve-month curriculum for single parents.

3. Shared in an interview at the Leadership Network seminar for pastors in churches of more than one thousand in worship, August, 1991.

4. "Churches That Care: Status Report #2 on Church-Housed Child Care," by Roger Neugebauer, *Exchange*, Sept./Oct. 1991, pp. 41-45.

5. For information on how to start a weekday child-care system, contact Colonial Hills United Methodist Church, 5247 Vance Jackson, San Antonio, Tex. 78230.

6. James Cobble, publisher of *Church Law and Tax Report*, cited in *National & International Religion Report*, September 7, 1992, p. 8.

7. Willow Creek Community Church uses *Promised Land* and Kensington Community Church uses *Treasure Island*.

8. *God Help Me Stop: Break Free from Addiction and Compulsion* (Glen Ellyn, Ill.: New Life Ministries), Box 343, Glen Ellyn, Ill. 60138.

9. For more information, see Nelle Morton, *The Journey Is Home* (Boston: Beacon Press, 1985); and Rosemary Radford Ruether, *Sexism and God-Talk: Toward a Feminist Theology* (Boston: Beacon Press, 1983).

10. Richard Ostling, "Strains on the Heart," *Time*, November 19, 1990, p. 88.

11. Lovers Lane United Methodist Church, Dallas, Texas. The Reverend Thomas Shipp was the pastor.

12. For more information, see William M. Easum, *How to Reach Baby Boomers* (Nashville: Abingdon Press, 1991).

Chapter 8. Three Essential Ingredients of Paradigm Communities

1. North Americans are becoming more conservative. We must understand and be able to converse with conservatives even if we may not be conservatives.

2. Church Information Development Services provides the most thorough demographic study prepared solely for use by religious organizations. In addition to the demographics contained in the census data, it provides physiographic and ethos data. One of the most thorough analyses of this information was done by Dr. Stanley Menking. He took the CIDS material and combined it with the VALS study and the material in Tex Sample's book, *U.S. Lifestyles and Mainline Churches* (Louisville: Westminster/John Knox Press, 1990). For more information, you may write Stanley Menking at Perkins School of Theology, Southern Methodist University, Office of Continuing Education, Dallas, Texas 75275 or call 1-214-768-2251.

3. Some of the best material I have seen on this topic is produced by Kensington Community Church in Kensington, Michigan.

4. The recent continuing study on baptism by The United Methodist Church is an example of a denomination going the wrong way. Instead of down-playing or eliminating infant baptism the denomination is trying to make provisions for all baptized infants to be considered members of the church. This is a subtle return to the Constantinian practice of mass baptism. The attempt shows how poorly many United Methodists understand the importance of personal experience among the generations born after World War II.

5. Celia Allison Hahn, foreword for Daniel V. Biles, *Pursuing Excellence in Ministry* (New York: Alban Institute, 1988).